OFFICIAL
Instant Pot
BOOK

The "I LOVE MY INSTANT POT®"
Recipe Book

From *Trail Mix Oatmeal* to *Mongolian Beef BBQ*,
175 Easy and Delicious Recipes

Michelle Fagone
of CavegirlCuisine.com

Adams Media

New York   London   Toronto   Sydney   New Delhi

To all of my fellow busy parents and home chefs . . . you got this!

Much love to the three nuts at my home—Sam, Samantha, and Calla—
that make all of this madness worth everything.

xo, Cavegirl, Michelle, and Mom

Adams media

Adams Media
An Imprint of Simon & Schuster, Inc.
57 Littlefield Street
Avon, Massachusetts 02322

This Adams Media trade paperback edition September 2019. First published in April 2017.

ADAMS MEDIA and colophon are trademarks of Simon & Schuster.

For information about special discounts for bulk purchases, please contact Simon & Schuster Special Sales at 1-866-506-1949 or business@simonandschuster.com.

The Simon & Schuster Speakers Bureau can bring authors to your live event. For more information or to book an event contact the Simon & Schuster Speakers Bureau at 1-866-248-3049 or visit our website at www.simonspeakers.com.

Interior design by Colleen Cunningham
Photographs by James Stefiuk

Manufactured in the United States of America

10 9 8 7 6 5 4 3

ISBN 978-1-5072-1280-6
ISBN 978-1-5072-1281-3 (ebook)

INSTANT POT® and associated logos are owned by Instant Brands Inc. and are used under license.

Always follow safety and commonsense cooking protocol while using kitchen utensils, operating ovens and stoves, and handling uncooked food. If children are assisting in the preparation of any recipe, they should always be supervised by an adult.

Contains material adapted from the following titles published by Adams Media, an Imprint of Simon & Schuster, Inc.: *The Everything® Pressure Cooker Cookbook* by Pamela Rice Hahn, copyright © 2009, ISBN 978-1-4405-0017-6; *The Everything® Vegetarian Pressure Cooker Cookbook* by Amy Snyder and Justin Snyder, copyright © 2010, ISBN 978-1-4405-0672-7; *The New Pressure Cooker Cookbook* by Adams Media, copyright © 2016, ISBN 978-1-4405-9749-7.

Contents

Introduction

The Instant Pot®.

Today everyone seems to have one, but you may not know what it can do, what to expect, or even what an Instant Pot® actually is. If that sounds familiar, don't worry. Throughout *The "I Love My Instant Pot®" Recipe Book*, you'll learn everything you need to know about this appliance and how and why you should use it.

Cooking with an Instant Pot® is life changing. Why? Because it is a multi-function cooking appliance. It is a pressure cooker, a rice cooker, a slow cooker, a yogurt maker, and even a sauté pan all rolled into one. It's a sleek dish that also allows you to sauté, brown, steam, and warm your food. It cooks soups, eggs, and even cheesecakes! And the high-pressure cooking and steaming ability of an Instant Pot® does wonders to steaks, pork shoulders, and chicken. These modern, cutting-edge workhorses are sleek, efficient, and easy to operate. With just the touch of a button, the Instant Pot® makes preparing a meal easier, cutting down cooking time from hours to minutes. In addition, the Instant Pot® actually cooks food at a lower temperature but it does it more efficiently than other methods because the pressure denies steam to release. This cooking method seals in essential vitamins and minerals and allows the Instant Pot® to turn out healthier, better-tasting food that is perfect when you're on the go. If you're worried about safety, don't be. Today's Instant Pot®s have several certified safety mechanisms in place. Depending on which Instant Pot® model you buy, the available safety features include a safety lid lock, pressure regulator, leaky lid smart detection, anti-blockage vent, power fuse cut-off, and more. These safety measures take the worry out of pressure cooking.

So whether you just brought your first Instant Pot® home today or have been using one for years, throughout the book you'll find 175 delicious dishes ranging from Southern Cheesy Grits and Steamed Bread Pudding, to Lemongrass Chicken and Lobster Risotto. The more you cook, the more you'll realize how versatile the Instant Pot® really is, whether you're making a hearty breakfast, an amazing main course, or a delicious dessert.

In this book, you'll find everything you need to know about how to use your Instant Pot®, including how to clean it, how to use the buttons, and what you should have on hand to make your dishes even better. You'll also notice that some of the recipes throughout the book are dedicated to paleo and gluten-free eating. If you have a family member with celiac disease, are avoiding carbs, or just want to dip your toes into the paleo and/or gluten-free waters without completely committing to the lifestyle, there are plenty of recipes that are perfect for you. So plug in your Instant Pot® and get ready to enjoy some amazing, quick meals.

Cooking with an Instant Pot®

So you're about to venture into the amazing world of Instant Pot® cooking . . . but you're not sure where or how to start. Don't worry, this chapter will give you the information that you need to know to get cooking. Here you'll learn what all those buttons on your Instant Pot® do, how to release the pressure from the Instant Pot® when your cooking time is up, how to keep your Instant Pot® clean, and more.

Even though you'll learn all this information in this chapter, it's so important that you read the owner's manual as well. The user manual is your key to successfully creating the recipes throughout this book. In addition to pointing out the basic functions of the appliance, it will tell you to do an initial test run using water to get familiar with the Instant Pot®. I can't stress enough that you need to do this. It will familiarize you with this appliance and take some of the anxiety away. In addition, this first run will help steam-clean your pot before you use it on a favorite recipe.

But for now, let's take a look at some Instant Pot® basics.

Function Buttons

You are staring at the Instant Pot® and there are so many buttons. Which one should you use? Although most of the function buttons seem obvious, several are set at pre-programmed default cooking times. And for every option, the Instant Pot® starts cooking 10 seconds after you hit the button. Mostly likely, you will utilize the Manual button the most because you are in complete control, but read on for more detailed information on the remaining function buttons.

Manual button. This might be your most used button on the Instant Pot®. The default pressure setting is High; however, you can toggle the pressure from High to Low by pressing the Pressure button. Use the Plus and Minus buttons to adjust the pressurized cooking time.

Sauté button. This button helps the Instant Pot® act as a skillet for sautéing vegetables or searing meat prior to adding the remaining ingredients of a recipe, and it is used for simmering sauces as well. There are three temperature settings—Normal, Less, and More—that can be accessed using the Adjust button. The Normal setting is for sautéing, the Less setting is for simmering, and the More setting is for searing meat. Keep the lid open when using the Sauté button to avoid pressure building up.

Soup button. This button is used to cook soups and broths at high pressure for a default of 30 minutes. The Adjust button allows you to change the cooking time to 20 or 40 minutes.

Porridge button. This button is used to cook porridge, congee, and jook in the Instant Pot® at high pressure for a default of 20 minutes. The Adjust button allows you to change the cooking time to 15 or 40 minutes.

Poultry button. This button is used to cook chicken, turkey, and even duck at high pressure for a default of 15 minutes. The Adjust button allows you to change the cooking time to 5 or 30 minutes.

Meat/Stew button. This button is used to cook red meats and chunky meat stews at high pressure for a default of 35 minutes. The Adjust button allows you to change the cooking time to 20 or 45 minutes.

Bean/Chili button. This button is used to cook dried beans and chili at high pressure for a default of 30 minutes. The Adjust button allows you to change the cooking time to 25 or 40 minutes.

Rice button. This button is used to cook white rice such as jasmine or basmati at low pressure. The Instant Pot® will automatically set the default cooking time by sensing the amount of water and rice that are in the cooking vessel.

Multigrain button. This button is used to cook grains such as wild rice, quinoa, and barley at high pressure for a default of 40 minutes. The Adjust button allows

you to change the cooking time to 20 or 60 minutes.

Steam button. This button is excellent for steaming veggies and seafood using your steamer basket. It steams for a default of 10 minutes. The Adjust button allows you to change the cooking time to 3 or 15 minutes. Quick-release the steam immediately after the timer beeps so as to not overcook the food.

Slow Cook button. This button allows the Instant Pot® to cook like a slow cooker. It defaults to a 4-hour cook time. The Adjust button allows you to change the temperature to Less, Normal, or More, which correspond to a slow cooker's low, normal, or high. The Plus and Minus buttons allow you to manually adjust the cooking time.

Keep Warm/Cancel button. When the Instant Pot® is being programmed or in operation, pressing this button cancels the operation and returns the Instant Pot® to a standby state. When the Instant Pot® is in the standby state, pressing this button again activates the Keep Warm function.

Automatic Keep Warm function. After the ingredients in the Instant Pot® are finished cooking, the Instant Pot® automatically switches over to the Keep Warm function and will keep your food warm for up to 10 hours. This is perfect for large cuts of meat as well as soups, stews, and chili, allowing the spices and flavors to really marry together for an even better taste. The first digit on the LED display will show an "L" to indicate that the Instant Pot® is in the Keep Warm cycle, and the clock will count up from 0 seconds to 10 hours.

Timer button. This button allows you to delay the start of cooking up to 24 hours. After you select a cooking program and make any time adjustments, press the Timer button and use the Plus or Minus keys to enter the delayed hours; press the Timer button again and use the Plus or Minus keys to enter the delayed minutes. You can press the Keep Warm/Cancel button to cancel the timed delay. The Timer function doesn't work with Sauté, Yogurt, and Keep Warm functions.

Locking and Pressure Release Methods

Other than the Sauté function, where the lid should be off, or the Slow Cook or Keep Warm functions, where the lid can be on or off, most of the cooking you'll do in the Instant Pot® will be under pressure, which means you need to know how to lock the lid before pressurized cooking and how to safely release the pressure after cooking. Once your ingredients are in the inner pot of the Instant Pot®, to lock the lid put the lid on the Instant Pot® with the triangle mark on the lid aligned with the Unlocked mark on the side of the Instant Pot®'s rim. Then turn the lid 30 degrees clockwise until the triangle mark on the lid is aligned with the Locked mark on the rim. Turn the pointed end of the pressure release handle on top of the lid to the Sealing position. After your cooking program has ended or you've pressed the Keep Warm/Cancel button to end the cooking, there are two ways you can release the pressure:

Natural-release method. To naturally release the pressure, simply wait until the Instant Pot® has cooled sufficiently for all of the pressure to be released and the float valve drops, normally about 10–15 minutes. You can either unplug the Instant Pot® while the pressure naturally releases or allow the pressure to release while it is still on the Keep Warm function.

Quick-release method. The quick-release method stifles the cooking process and helps unlock the lid for immediate serving. To quickly release the pressure on the Instant Pot®, make sure you are wearing oven mitts, then turn the pressure release handle to the Venting position to let out steam until the float valve drops. This is generally not recommended for starchy items or large volumes of liquids (e.g., soup) so as to avoid any splattering that may occur. Be prepared, because the noise and geyser effect of the releasing steam experienced during the quick-release method can be off-putting. Also, if you own dogs, apparently this release is the most frightening part of the day so take caution.

Pot-In-Pot Accessories

Pot-in-pot cooking is when you place another cooking dish inside the Instant Pot® for a particular recipe. The Instant Pot® is straightforward and comes with an inner pot and trivet; however, there are many other tricks and recipes that can be made with the purchase of few other accessories, including a springform pan, cake pan, 7-cup glass bowl, and ramekins.

7" springform pan. A 7" springform pan is the perfect size for making a cheesecake in an Instant Pot®. It is the right dimension to fit inside the Instant Pot®, and it makes a cheesecake for four to six people.

6" cake pan. A 6" pan is excellent for making a small cake in the Instant Pot®. It can serve four to six people depending on the serving size. This pan is perfect for a family craving a small dessert without committing to leftovers.

7-cup glass bowl. This 7-cup bowl fits perfectly in the Instant Pot® and works great for eggs and bread puddings that generally would burn on the bottom of the insert. The items in the bowl sit up on the inserted trivet and are cooked with the steam and pressure of the pot.

Ramekins. These 4-ounce porcelain individual portions are nontoxic and environmentally friendly, providing the perfect vessel for tasty custards.

Steamer basket. The steamer basket helps create a lifted shelf for steaming. There is a choice of a metal or a silicone steamer. Shop around as there are several variations. Some even have handles already connected for ease of lifting after the cooking process.

Although these accessories help you branch out into different recipes that can be used with the Instant Pot®, there are many recipes using the inner pot and trivet that come with your appliance. The accessories are just a fun extension with what will soon become your favorite heat source in the kitchen.

Accessory Removal

Cooking pot-in-pot is a great idea until it's time to remove the inserted cooking dish. Because of the tight space, it is almost impossible to use thick oven mitts to reach down and grip something evenly without tipping one side of the cooking vessel and spilling the cooked item. There are a few ways around this:

Retriever tongs. Retriever tongs are a helpful tool for removing hot bowls and pans from the Instant Pot®.

Mini mitts. Silicone mini mitts are helpful when lifting pots out of an Instant Pot® after the cooking process. They are less cumbersome than traditional oven mitts, which can prove to be bulky in the tight space of the cooker.

Aluminum foil sling. This is a quick, inexpensive fix to the problem of lifting a heated dish out of an Instant Pot®. Take an approximate 10" × 10" square of aluminum foil and fold it back and forth until you have a 2" × 10" sling. Place this sling underneath the bowl or pan before cooking so that you can easily lift up the heated dish.

Although necessary if you do pot-in-pot cooking, these retrieval tools are not needed if you are simply using the interior pot that comes with the appliance upon purchase. A slotted spoon will do the trick for most other meals.

Cleaning Your Instant Pot®

When cleaning up after use, the first thing you should do is unplug the Instant Pot® and allow it to cool. Then you can break down the following parts to clean and inspect for any trapped food particles:

Inner pot. The inner pot, the cooking vessel, is dishwasher safe; however, the high heat causes rainbowing, or discoloration, on stainless steel. To avoid this, hand wash the pot.

Outer heating unit. Wipe the interior and exterior with a damp cloth. Do not submerge in water as it is an electrical appliance.

Trivet. The trivet is dishwasher safe or can be cleaned with soap and water.

Lid. The lid needs to be broken down into individual parts before washing. The sealing ring, the float valve, the steam release handle, and the anti-block shield all need to be cleaned in different ways:

- **Sealing ring.** Once this ring is removed, check the integrity of the silicone. If this ring is torn or cracked, it will not seal properly and may cause a hindrance to the cooking process and should not be used. The sealing ring needs to be removed and washed each time because the ring has a tendency to hold odors when cooking. Vinegar or lemon juice is excellent for reducing the odors. For a nominal price, additional rings can be purchased. Some use one ring for meats and a separate one for desserts and milder dishes.

- **Float valve.** The float valve is a safety feature that serves as a latch lock that prevents the lid from being opened during the cooking process. Make sure that this valve can move easily and is not obstructed by any food particles.

- **Pressure release handle.** This is the venting handle on top of the lid. It can be pulled out for cleaning. It should be loose so don't worry. This allows it to move when necessary.

- **Anti-block shield.** The anti-block shield is the little silver "basket" on the underneath side of the lid. It is located directly below the vent. This shield can and should be removed and cleaned. It blocks any foods, especially starches, so they don't clog the vent.

So, now that you know about all of the Instant Pot®'s safety features, function buttons, parts, and how to clean everything, it's time for the fun part. The cooking process is where the excitement begins. From breakfast to dessert and everything in between, *The "I Love My Instant Pot®" Recipe Book* has you covered.

2

Breakfast

Breakfast is the most important meal of the day, as they say. But a lot of people just don't have the time or energy to create a well-rounded plate of food. Most mornings you may just be too tired or too busy—or both. Fortunately, the Instant Pot® can help save the day with its shortened cooking time and freedom from having to stand over the skillet. All you have to do is add your ingredients, press a button, and go get ready to tackle your day. Try prepping some of the fruits and vegetables the night before, so you can eliminate this step in the morning as well. And when breakfast is ready, all you have to do is drop the interior cooker pot right into your dishwasher, alleviating that hassle of coming home to a stack of dirty dishes.

From grits to eggs, this chapter has got you covered with a myriad of delicious breakfast recipes, including Peachy Cream Oats, Southern Cheesy Grits, and Crustless Crab Quiche. And once you get comfortable with some of the basics, you should feel free to get creative and make some of your own morning masterpieces. So get cooking, and let your family wake up with a new appreciation for their soon-to-be-favorite kitchen gadget!

Southern Cheesy Grits

Yes, instant grits are quick, but the Instant Pot® allows you to cook stone-ground grits and polenta, or corn grits, in no time at all. And when it comes right down to it, there is no comparison. The real thing is always better.

- **Hands-On Time: 5 minutes**
- **Cook Time: 10 minutes**

Serves 4

¾ plus 1½ cups water, divided
1 cup stone-ground grits
2 tablespoons butter
1 teaspoon sea salt
½ teaspoon ground black pepper
½ cup grated sharp Cheddar cheese

INSTANT POT® OPTIONS
If you really want to pump up the volume on these grits, mix in some crumbled bacon and scrambled eggs. Serve a buttermilk biscuit on the side (and maybe some sweet tea) and you have just elevated yourself into an official Southern chef.

1. Place ¾ cup water in the bottom of the Instant Pot®. Insert the trivet.

2. In the stainless-steel bowl that fits down into the pot insert, stir together the grits, butter, remaining 1½ cups water, salt, and pepper. Lock lid.

3. Press the Rice button (the Instant Pot® will determine the cooking time, about 10 minutes pressurized cooking time). When timer beeps, quick-release the pressure until the float valve drops and then unlock the lid. Stir in the cheese and serve warm.

Sweet Potato Morning Hash

PALEO, GLUTEN-FREE

Whether you've just finished up a CrossFit class or finally managed to get your kids on the bus, you are starving. Let your Instant Pot® be your personal chef and cook this Sweet Potato Morning Hash while you are showering off and getting ready for your day. When ready, ladle a bowl of flavor-filled protein and veggies into your breakfast bowl to help you tackle the day.

- **Hands-On Time: 10 minutes**
- **Cook Time: 10 minutes**

Serves 4

6 large eggs

1 tablespoon Italian seasoning

½ teaspoon sea salt

½ teaspoon ground black pepper

½ pound ground pork sausage

1 large sweet potato, peeled and cubed

1 small onion, peeled and diced

2 cloves garlic, minced

1 medium green bell pepper, seeded and diced

2 cups water

1 In a medium bowl, whisk together eggs, Italian seasoning, salt, and pepper. Set aside.

2 Press the Sauté button on Instant Pot®. Stir-fry sausage, sweet potato, onion, garlic, and bell pepper for 3–5 minutes until onions are translucent.

3 Transfer mixture to a 7-cup greased glass dish. Pour whisked eggs over the sausage mixture.

4 Place trivet in Instant Pot®. Pour in water. Place dish with egg mixture onto trivet. Lock lid.

5 Press the Manual button and adjust time to 5 minutes. When timer beeps, quick-release pressure until float valve drops and then unlock lid. Remove dish from Instant Pot®. Let sit at room temperature for 5–10 minutes to allow the eggs to set. Slice and serve.

Bacon-Poblano Morning Taters

PALEO, GLUTEN-FREE

Enjoy these potatoes with a nice poached egg over the top. And if you really want to take this dish to the next level, drizzle some luxurious hollandaise over the egg.

- **Hands-On Time: 10 minutes**
- **Cook Time: 10 minutes**

Serves 4

1 tablespoon olive oil
2 slices bacon, diced
1 small onion, peeled and
   diced
2 small poblano peppers,
   seeded and diced
4 cups small-diced russet
   potatoes
2 tablespoons ghee
2–3 cloves garlic, minced
1 teaspoon sea salt
½ teaspoon ground black
   pepper
½ cup water

1 Press Sauté button on Instant Pot® and heat oil. Add bacon, onion, and peppers. Stir-fry until onions are translucent, 3–5 minutes. Transfer mixture to a 7-cup glass dish. Toss in potatoes, ghee, garlic, salt, and pepper.

2 Insert trivet into Instant Pot®. Pour in water. Place dish on trivet. Lock lid.

3 Press the Manual button and adjust time to 5 minutes. When the timer beeps, let the pressure release naturally until the float valve drops (about 10–15 minutes). Remove dish from pot and serve.

Sunday Brunch Sausage Gravy

If biscuits and gravy are your favorite breakfast, then this Sunday Brunch Sausage Gravy is going to knock your socks off. Show off your cooking skills by making this for a holiday brunch for your family and guests. And even though this gravy is so good you'll want to eat it by the spoonful, don't forget to bring the biscuits.

- **Hands-On Time: 5 minutes**
- **Cook Time: 10 minutes**

Serves 10

2 tablespoons butter

1 pound ground pork sausage

1 small sweet onion, peeled and diced

¼ cup chicken broth

¼ cup all-purpose flour

1½ cups heavy cream

½ teaspoon sea salt

1 tablespoon ground black pepper

1 Press the Sauté button on the Instant Pot®. Add butter and heat until melted. Add pork sausage and onion. Stir-fry 3–5 minutes until onions are translucent. The pork will still be a little pink in places. Add chicken broth. Lock lid.

2 Press the Manual button and adjust time to 1 minute. When the timer beeps, quick-release the pressure until the float valve drops and then unlock the lid. Whisk in flour, cream, salt, and pepper.

3 Press the Keep Warm button and let the gravy sit for about 5–10 minutes to allow the sauce to thicken. Remove from heat and serve warm.

Nuts and Fruit Oatmeal

Instead of plain old oatmeal, wake up happy to this bowl of flavors and warmth that will have you doing a jig out the door—no matter the weather. This dish is absolutely perfect for a cold morning when you just need a little extra get-up-and-go. This recipe calls for dried cherries, but you can use whatever dried fruit you prefer. And if you'd like, feel free to top this dish with milk and additional sweetener, if necessary.

- **Hands-On Time: 5 minutes**
- **Cook Time: 7 minutes**

Serves 2

1 cup old-fashioned oats
1¼ cups water
¼ cup freshly squeezed orange juice
1 medium pear, peeled, cored, and cubed
¼ cup dried cherries
¼ cup chopped walnuts
1 tablespoon honey
¼ teaspoon ground ginger
¼ teaspoon ground cinnamon
Pinch of salt

INSTANT POT® OPTIONS

If you'd like, use an apple instead of the pear. Also, there are many dried fruits sold such as raisins, cranberries, pineapple, and many more that you can experiment with.

1 In the Instant Pot® bowl, add the oats, water, orange juice, pear, cherries, walnuts, honey, ginger, cinnamon, and salt. Stir to combine. Lock lid.

2 Press the Manual button and adjust time to 7 minutes. When the timer beeps, let pressure release naturally until the float valve drops and then unlock the lid.

3 Stir oatmeal and spoon the cooked oats into two bowls. Serve warm.

Banana Nut Bread Oatmeal

This oatmeal will flood back memories of Grandma's banana bread, but with a healthy twist. Bananas are high in potassium. Walnuts contain anti-inflammatory omega-3 essential fatty acids. And cinnamon, the underrated spice of the decade, contains manganese and fiber and is an excellent source of calcium. If you'd like, feel free to top this dish with additional milk and sweetener, if necessary.

- **Hands-On Time: 5 minutes**
- **Cook Time: 7 minutes**

Serves 2

1 cup old-fashioned oats

1 cup water

1 cup whole milk

2 ripe bananas, peeled and sliced

2 tablespoons pure maple syrup

2 teaspoons ground cinnamon

¼ teaspoon vanilla extract

2 tablespoons chopped walnuts

Pinch of salt

1   In the Instant Pot® bowl, add the oats, water, milk, bananas, maple syrup, cinnamon, vanilla, walnuts, and salt. Stir to combine. Lock lid.

2   Press the Manual button and adjust time to 7 minutes. When the timer beeps, let pressure release naturally until float valve drops and then unlock lid.

3   Stir oatmeal. Spoon the cooked oats into two bowls. Serve warm.

Trail Mix Oatmeal

This oatmeal, packed full of nuts, fruit, and flavor, will get you ready for the hiking trail. It will also see you out the door with some serious nutritional benefits even if you're heading to the office and not the woods. So breathe in that fresh air and enjoy the beautiful morning. And don't worry; this breakfast is hearty and will keep you full until lunch. Feel free to top this oatmeal with milk, additional sweetener, and blackberries and raspberries if desired.

- **Hands-On Time: 5 minutes**
- **Cook Time: 10 minutes**

Serves 2

1 cup steel-cut oats

1½ cups water

2 teaspoons butter

1 cup (from 1 large orange) freshly squeezed orange juice

1 tablespoon dried cranberries

1 tablespoon raisins

1 tablespoon chopped dried apricots

2 tablespoons pure maple syrup

¼ teaspoon ground cinnamon

2 tablespoons chopped pecans

Pinch of salt

1 Add all ingredients to the Instant Pot® bowl and stir to combine. Lock lid.

2 Press the Manual button and adjust time to 10 minutes. When timer beeps, quick-release pressure until float valve drops and then unlock lid.

3 Stir oatmeal. Spoon the cooked oats into two bowls. Serve warm.

Peachy Cream Oats

Make sure you use ripe peaches in this morning oat delight to take advantage of the natural sugars in ripe fruit. Also, this recipe is an excellent summer and early fall breakfast choice as peaches are in their peak season. You may also want to experiment with different varieties. The doughnut peach is not only unique in shape but is quite sweet and juicy.

- **Hands-On Time: 5 minutes**
- **Cook Time: 7 minutes**

Serves 2

1 cup old-fashioned oats
1 cup water
1 cup whole milk
4 ripe peaches, peeled, pitted, and diced
2 tablespoons packed light brown sugar
¼ teaspoon vanilla extract
2 tablespoons chopped pecans
Pinch of salt

1 In the Instant Pot® bowl, add the oats, water, milk, peaches, brown sugar, vanilla, pecans, and salt. Stir to combine. Lock lid.

2 Press the Manual button and adjust time to 7 minutes. When timer beeps, quick-release pressure until float valve drops and then unlock lid.

3 Stir oatmeal. Spoon the cooked oats into two bowls. Serve warm.

Tex-Mex Breakfast

This breakfast is hearty enough for a late-night meal or snack and easy enough to prepare. Let your Instant Pot® take the lead, then cuddle back up in bed and binge-watch that show you've been dying to see.

- **Hands-On Time: 15 minutes**
- **Cook Time: 10 minutes**

Serves 4

6 large eggs
½ teaspoon sea salt
¼ teaspoon ground black pepper
⅛ teaspoon chili powder
½ cup shredded Cheddar cheese
1 small Roma tomato, diced
2 tablespoons butter
2 small (or 1 large) Yukon gold potatoes, grated
2 cups cubed cooked ham
1 small onion, peeled and diced
1 small jalapeño, seeded and diced
½ cup sliced button mushrooms
2 cups water

1 In a medium bowl, whisk together eggs, salt, pepper, and chili powder. Stir in cheese and tomato. Set aside.

2 Press the Sauté button on Instant Pot®. Heat the butter and stir-fry potatoes, ham, onion, jalapeño, and mushrooms for approximately 5 minutes until the potatoes are tender and onions are translucent.

3 Transfer cooked mixture to a 7-cup greased glass dish. Pour whisked eggs over the potato mixture.

4 Place trivet in Instant Pot®. Pour in water. Place dish with egg mixture onto trivet. Lock lid.

5 Press the Manual button and adjust time to 5 minutes. When timer beeps, quick-release pressure until float valve drops and then unlock lid.

6 Remove dish from the Instant Pot®. Let sit at room temperature for 5–10 minutes to allow the eggs to set. Slice and serve warm.

Brunchy Sausage Bowl

The saltiness of the pork sausage and the creaminess of the corn used in this recipe just spells love. This is a one-pot wonder gone magical, and the whole family will beg you to make it every weekend. And since it's so easy, you'll happily oblige.

- **Hands-On Time: 10 minutes**
- **Cook Time: 10 minutes**

Serves 4

1 pound pork sausage links

2 large potatoes, peeled and thinly sliced

1 medium red bell pepper, seeded and diced

1 medium sweet onion, peeled and diced

1 (16-ounce) can creamed corn

½ teaspoon sea salt

¼ teaspoon ground black pepper

¾ cup tomato juice

INSTANT POT® OPTIONS

This dish can be dressed up with fresh parsley, diced tomatoes, avocado slices, and shredded cheese.

1 Press the Sauté button on Instant Pot®. Add sausage links and brown for 4–5 minutes. Move the sausages to a plate.

2 Layer the potatoes, bell pepper, onion, and corn in the Instant Pot®. Sprinkle with salt and pepper. Place sausage links on top of the corn. Pour the tomato juice over the top of the other ingredients in the Instant Pot®. Lock lid.

3 Press the Manual button and adjust time to 5 minutes. When the timer beeps, let the pressure release naturally for at least 10 minutes.

4 Quick-release any additional pressure until the float valve drops and then unlock lid. Serve warm.

California Frittata Bake

Fresh and light and healthy, this breakfast frittata will have you feeling that warm California breeze in your hair. Packed with fresh, healthy ingredients, this Instant Pot® recipe is guaranteed to get you California dreaming in no time flat.

- **Hands-On Time: 10 minutes**
- **Cook Time: 10 minutes**

Serves 4

4 large eggs
4 large egg whites
½ teaspoon sea salt
¼ teaspoon ground black pepper
¼ cup chopped fresh basil
½ cup chopped spinach
2 small Roma tomatoes, diced
1 medium avocado, pitted and diced
¼ cup grated Gruyère cheese
1 tablespoon avocado oil
1 pound ground chicken
1 small onion, peeled and diced
1 cup water

1 In a medium bowl, whisk together eggs, egg whites, salt, and pepper. Add basil, spinach, tomatoes, avocado, and cheese. Set aside.

2 Press the Sauté button on Instant Pot®. Heat the avocado oil and stir-fry chicken and onion for approximately 5 minutes or until chicken is no longer pink.

3 Transfer cooked mixture to a 7-cup greased glass dish and set aside to cool. Once cool pour whisked eggs over the chicken mixture and stir to combine.

4 Place trivet in Instant Pot®. Pour in water. Place dish with egg mixture onto trivet. Lock lid.

5 Press the Manual button and adjust time to 5 minutes. When the timer beeps, let pressure release naturally until the float valve drops and then unlock the lid.

6 Remove dish from the Instant Pot® and set aside for 5–10 minutes to allow the eggs to set. Slice and serve.

Chocolate Banana French Toast Casserole

Is it breakfast or is it dessert? Fortunately, it's both so you can satisfy that sweet tooth and still get your morning started right. Perfect for overnight holiday guests or even after a birthday slumber party, this dish is fantastic with a dollop of fresh whipped cream for a little extra treat.

- **Hands-On Time: 10 minutes**
- **Cook Time: 20 minutes**

Serves 4

4 cups cubed bread, dried out overnight, divided

2 bananas, peeled and sliced

4 tablespoons chocolate syrup, divided

2 cups whole milk

3 large eggs

1 teaspoon vanilla extract

¼ cup pure maple syrup

Pinch of ground nutmeg

Pinch of sea salt

3 tablespoons butter, cut into 3 pats

1 cup water

1 Grease a 7-cup glass dish. Add 2 cups bread. Arrange banana slices in an even layer over bread. Drizzle 2 tablespoons chocolate syrup over bananas. Add remaining 2 cups bread. Set aside.

2 In a medium bowl, whisk together milk, eggs, vanilla, maple syrup, nutmeg, and salt. Pour over bread; place pats of butter on top.

3 Pour water into Instant Pot®. Set trivet in Instant Pot®. Place glass dish on top of trivet. Lock lid.

4 Press the Manual button and adjust time to 20 minutes. When the timer beeps, quick-release pressure until float valve drops and then unlock lid.

5 Remove glass bowl from the Instant Pot®. Transfer to a rack until cooled. Top with remaining 2 tablespoons chocolate. Serve warm.

Strawberry Cream–Filled French Toast Casserole

Creamy and sweet, indulgent and zesty, this casserole will have your taste buds screaming for more. And don't let your oranges go to waste after zesting. Instead, juice them! Oranges are not only an excellent source of vitamin C but are high in dietary fiber.

- **Hands-On Time: 15 minutes**
- **Cook Time: 20 minutes**

Serves 4

8 ounces cream cheese, room temperature

¼ cup sugar

2 cups sliced strawberries

1 tablespoon orange zest

4 cups cubed bread, dried out overnight, divided

2 cups whole milk

3 large eggs

1 teaspoon vanilla extract

¼ cup pure maple syrup

Pinch of ground nutmeg

Pinch of sea salt

3 tablespoons butter, cut into 3 pats

1 cup water

4 teaspoons powdered sugar

1 In a large bowl, cream together the cream cheese and sugar by mashing ingredients with the tines of a fork. Fold in strawberries and orange zest. Set aside.

2 Grease a 7-cup glass dish. Add 2 cups bread. Spoon in a layer of the strawberry mixture. Add remaining 2 cups bread. Set aside.

3 In a medium bowl, whisk together milk, eggs, vanilla, maple syrup, nutmeg, and salt. Pour over bread; place pats of butter on top.

4 Pour water into Instant Pot®. Set trivet in Instant Pot®. Place glass dish on top of trivet. Lock lid.

5 Press the Manual button and adjust time to 20 minutes. When the timer beeps, quick-release pressure until float valve drops and then unlock lid.

6 Remove glass bowl from the Instant Pot®. Transfer to a rack until cooled. Sprinkle with powdered sugar.

Pumpkin Spice Latte French Toast Casserole

If you love pumpkin spice, now you can have your latte and eat it, too. Don't miss out on the craze just because you don't drink coffee. Make this morning treat and see for yourself what all of the fuss is about.

- **Hands-On Time: 15 minutes**
- **Cook Time: 20 minutes**

Serves 4

4 cups cubed whole-wheat bread

1½ cups whole milk

¼ cup brewed coffee, cooled

3 large eggs

¼ cup pumpkin purée

1 teaspoon vanilla extract

¼ cup pure maple syrup

2 teaspoons pumpkin pie spice

Pinch of sea salt

3 tablespoons butter, cut into 3 pats

1 cup water

1 Grease a 7-cup glass dish. Add bread. Set aside.

2 In a medium bowl, whisk together milk, coffee, eggs, pumpkin purée, vanilla, maple syrup, pumpkin pie spice, and salt. Pour over bread; place pats of butter on top.

3 Pour water into Instant Pot®. Set trivet in Instant Pot®. Place glass dish on top of trivet. Lock lid.

4 Press the Manual button and adjust time to 20 minutes. When the timer beeps, quick-release the pressure until float valve drops and then unlock lid.

5 Remove glass bowl from the Instant Pot®. Transfer to a rack until cool. Serve.

INSTANT POT® OPTIONS
If you'd like, feel free to finish off this casserole with any number of toppings. Serve it with powdered sugar or fresh whipped cream. You can also substitute pumpkin butter for the regular pats of butter to really drive home this dish's pumpkin power.

Western Omelet Casserole

Among many theories and tall tales, the western omelet is said to have been given its name because cowpokes had the ingredients needed to make it when they were out on a cattle drive. After becoming accustomed to this meal, the cowboys started to request these omelets in larger western cities, such as Denver, where it is now also called a Denver omelet.

- **Hands-On Time: 5 minutes**
- **Cook Time: 10 minutes**

Serves 4

6 large eggs
½ teaspoon sea salt
½ teaspoon ground black pepper
2 dashes hot sauce
1 cup diced ham
1 small red bell pepper, seeded and diced
1 small green bell pepper, seeded and diced
1 small onion, peeled and diced
2 cups water

1 In a medium bowl, whisk together eggs, salt, pepper, and hot sauce. Set aside.

2 Press the Sauté button on Instant Pot®. Stir-fry ham, bell peppers, and onion for 3–5 minutes or until onions are translucent.

3 Transfer mixture to a greased 7-cup glass dish. Pour whisked eggs over the ham mixture.

4 Place trivet in Instant Pot®. Pour in water. Place dish with egg mixture onto trivet. Lock lid.

5 Press the Manual button and adjust time to 5 minutes. When timer beeps, quick-release pressure until float valve drops and then unlock lid.

6 Remove dish from the Instant Pot®. Let sit at room temperature for 5–10 minutes to allow the eggs to set. Slice and serve.

Crustless Crab Quiche

PALEO, GLUTEN-FREE

This brunch item is screaming to be plated with a thick slice of tomato, some fresh thyme, and a few avocado wedges. In no time, you can serve this elegant breakfast in bed with a couple of mimosas (with freshly squeezed orange juice, of course) for you and the one that you love to enjoy.

- **Hands-On Time: 10 minutes**
- **Cook Time: 10 minutes**

Serves 6

6 large eggs

¼ cup unsweetened almond milk

2 teaspoons fresh thyme leaves

½ teaspoon sea salt

¼ teaspoon ground black pepper

½ teaspoon hot sauce

½ pound crabmeat

¼ cup crumbled goat cheese

2 thick slices bacon, diced

¼ cup peeled and diced onion

¼ cup seeded and diced green bell pepper

2 cups water

1. In a medium bowl, whisk eggs, milk, thyme leaves, salt, pepper, and hot sauce. Stir in crabmeat and goat cheese. Set aside.

2. Grease a 7-cup glass dish. Set aside.

3. Press the Sauté button on Instant Pot®. Add diced bacon and brown for 2 minutes, rendering some fat. Add onion and bell pepper and stir-fry with bacon until tender. Transfer mixture to the glass container. Pour in egg mixture.

4. Place trivet in Instant Pot®. Pour in water. Place dish with egg mixture onto trivet. Lock lid.

5. Press the Manual button and adjust time to 5 minutes. When timer beeps, let pressure release naturally for 10 minutes. Quick-release any additional pressure until float valve drops and then unlock lid.

6. Remove dish from Instant Pot®. Let cool for 10 minutes to allow eggs to set. Slice and serve.

Egg Muffins to Go

Mornings are busy. Maybe you're rushing to get to work, to get to the gym, or to get your kids onto the bus on time. If your morning is spent running around, these handy Egg Muffins to Go made in no time at all in the Instant Pot® make it easy to get a quick veggie-filled, protein-packed bite on your way out the door.

- **Hands-On Time: 10 minutes**
- **Cook Time: 15 minutes**

Serves 3

1 tablespoon olive oil

3 pieces bacon, diced

1 small onion, peeled and diced

4 large eggs

2 teaspoons Italian seasoning

½ teaspoon sea salt

½ teaspoon ground black pepper

¼ cup shredded Cheddar cheese

1 small Roma tomato, diced

¼ cup chopped spinach

1 cup water

1 Press the Sauté button on Instant Pot®. Heat olive oil. Add bacon and onion and stir-fry 3–5 minutes until onions are translucent. Transfer mixture to a small bowl to cool.

2 In a medium bowl, whisk together eggs, Italian seasoning, salt, black pepper, cheese, tomatoes, and spinach. Stir in cooled bacon mixture.

3 Place trivet into Instant Pot®. Pour in water. Place steamer basket on trivet.

4 Distribute egg mixture evenly among 6 silicone muffin cups. Carefully place cups on steamer basket. Lock lid.

5 Press the Manual button and adjust time to 8 minutes. When the timer beeps, quick-release pressure until float valve drops and then unlock lid.

6 Remove egg muffins and serve warm.

Ham and Swiss Muffin Frittatas

These Ham and Swiss Muffin Frittatas feature a traditional combination of classic flavors. If you want to take these muffin frittatas up a notch, trade out the ham and cheese for prosciutto and Gruyère cheese, and swap out the red bell pepper for some diced asparagus.

- **Hands-On Time: 10 minutes**
- **Cook Time: 15 minutes**

Serves 3

1 tablespoon olive oil

¼ cup small-diced ham

¼ cup diced red bell pepper, seeded

4 large eggs

½ teaspoon sea salt

½ teaspoon ground black pepper

¼ cup shredded Swiss cheese

1 cup water

1 Press the Sauté button on Instant Pot®. Heat olive oil. Add ham and bell pepper and stir-fry 3–5 minutes until peppers are tender. Transfer mixture to a small bowl to cool.

2 In a medium bowl, whisk together eggs, salt, pepper, and Swiss cheese. Stir in cooled ham mixture.

3 Place trivet into Instant Pot®. Pour in water. Place steamer basket on trivet.

4 Distribute egg mixture evenly among 6 silicone muffin cups. Carefully place cups on steamer basket. Lock lid.

5 Press the Manual button and adjust time to 8 minutes. When timer beeps, quick-release pressure until float valve drops and then unlock lid.

6 Remove frittatas and serve warm.

3

Soups

Sometimes you may have all of the ingredients for a great soup, but you look at the clock and realize you are only an hour out from dinner. Traditionally, you've needed low heat and a long cooking time to marry together all of the wonderful spices and flavors that make any soup great, but not anymore. The pressurized heat in your Instant Pot® can save the day. Although there is a Slow Cook button on your Instant Pot® for when time isn't an issue, cooking at high pressure can have you serving a finished dinner within an hour. To cut back on time even more, you can find precut onions and peppers in the freezer section of your local grocery store that work great in a pinch. So break out your ladle because dinner is almost ready.

Chicken Broth

PALEO, GLUTEN-FREE

Don't skip this recipe after you cook a whole chicken or purchase a cooked rotisserie chicken from the supermarket. Save the carcass and bones to make this nutrient- and mineral-packed Chicken Broth that you can use for a soup base in place of store-bought stock.

- **Hands-On Time: 10 minutes**
- **Cook Time: 30 minutes**

Yields 6 cups

1 chicken carcass from a whole chicken

2 large carrots, peeled and cut into chunks

2 stalks celery, cut into chunks

1 small onion, peeled and chopped

1 bay leaf

2 cloves garlic, peeled and halved

½ teaspoon apple cider vinegar

1 teaspoon sea salt

6 cups water

1 Place all ingredients into the Instant Pot®. Press the Manual button and adjust time to 30 minutes. When timer beeps, let pressure release naturally until float valve drops and then unlock lid.

2 Use a slotted spoon to retrieve and discard any large items from the broth. Strain the remaining liquid through a fine sieve or cheesecloth. Refrigerate broth for up to 4 days or freeze for up to 6 months.

Vegetable Broth

PALEO, GLUTEN-FREE

Broths are the base, the very foundation, of almost any soup that you make, so feel free to alter this recipe in order to personalize the flavor of the broth. For example, if you know a guest dislikes garlic, then make this broth without it. If you have everything but the parsnip, eliminate it. Tailor this broth to your own taste buds and preferences as well. It will be amazing!

- **Hands-On Time: 10 minutes**
- **Cook Time: 30 minutes**

Yields 6 cups

3 large carrots, peeled and cut into chunks

2 stalks celery, cut into chunks

1 small onion, peeled and chopped

1 medium parsnip, peeled and chopped

1 bay leaf

2 cloves garlic, peeled and halved

½ teaspoon apple cider vinegar

1 teaspoon sea salt

6 cups water

1 Place all ingredients into the Instant Pot®. Lock lid.

2 Press the Manual button and adjust time to 30 minutes. When timer beeps, let pressure release naturally until float valve drops and then unlock lid.

3 Use a slotted spoon to retrieve and discard any large items from the broth. Strain the remaining liquid through a fine sieve or cheesecloth. Refrigerate broth for up to 4 days or freeze for up to 6 months.

Beef Broth

PALEO, GLUTEN-FREE

Beef soup bones can be bought at most supermarkets and butcher shops. If they are not on display, don't hesitate to ask. Making your own beef and bone broth is very popular these days, so it won't seem like a weird question. You can also use oxtail or neck bones as a substitute.

- **Hands-On Time: 10 minutes**
- **Cook Time: 30 minutes**

Yields 6 cups

3 pounds beef soup bones

2 large carrots, peeled and cut into chunks

2 stalks celery, cut into chunks

1 small onion, peeled and chopped

1 bay leaf

2 cloves garlic, peeled and halved

½ teaspoon apple cider vinegar

1 teaspoon sea salt

6 cups water

1 Place all ingredients into the Instant Pot®. Lock lid.

2 Press the Manual button and adjust time to 30 minutes. When timer beeps, let pressure release naturally until float valve drops and then unlock lid.

3 Use a slotted spoon to retrieve and discard any large items from the broth. Strain the remaining liquid through a fine sieve or cheesecloth. Refrigerate broth for up to 4 days or freeze for up to 6 months.

Spicy Chicken Chili

When the air starts getting crisp, this Spicy Chicken Chili should be in your Instant Pot®. This warmth-inducing, crowd-pleasing dish will have your friends asking if they can watch the game at your house every weekend. And not only will you have the winning dish of the day, but you will actually get to visit with your guests instead of being stuck in the kitchen cooking. Let your Instant Pot® do all of the work!

- **Hands-On Time: 15 minutes**
- **Cook Time: 40 minutes**

Serves 8

1 tablespoon olive oil

1 pound ground chicken

1 medium yellow onion, peeled and diced

3 cloves garlic, minced

3 canned chipotle chilies in adobo sauce

1 (15-ounce) can dark red kidney beans, drained and rinsed

1 (15-ounce) can black beans, drained and rinsed

1 teaspoon Worcestershire sauce

1 (30-ounce) can diced tomatoes, including liquid

1 (4-ounce) can diced green chilies, including liquid

1 teaspoon sea salt

2 teaspoons hot sauce

1 teaspoon smoked paprika

1 teaspoon chili powder

1 Press the Sauté button on the Instant Pot®. Heat oil. Add the ground chicken and onion and stir-fry approximately 5 minutes until chicken is no longer pink.

2 Stir in the remaining ingredients. Lock lid.

3 Press the Meat button and cook for the default time of 35 minutes.

4 When timer beeps, let pressure release naturally until float valve drops and then unlock lid.

5 Ladle into individual bowls and serve warm.

INSTANT POT® OPTIONS

Let your guests choose what to garnish their bowls of chili with by presenting options such as sour cream, diced onions, shredded cheese, and fresh cilantro.

Beanless Chili

PALEO, GLUTEN-FREE

Some think that a good chili recipe needs to include beans. Some argue otherwise. No matter which side of the argument you fall on, this delicious Beanless Chili will make you forget about the whole bean dilemma! This dish is warm, comforting, and only takes about an hour to make. What could be better than that?

- **Hands-On Time: 10 minutes**
- **Cook Time: 40 minutes**

Serves 4

1 tablespoon olive oil
½ pound ground pork
½ pound ground beef
1 medium onion, peeled and diced
1 small green bell pepper, seeded and diced
1 large carrot, peeled and diced
3 cloves garlic, minced
2 tablespoons chili powder
1 teaspoon sea salt
2 teaspoons ground black pepper
1 small jalapeño, seeded and diced
1 (28-ounce) can puréed tomatoes (including juice)

1 Press the Sauté button on the Instant Pot®. Heat oil. Add the ground pork, ground beef, and onion. Stir-fry for 5 minutes until pork is no longer pink.

2 Add remaining ingredients. Lock lid.

3 Press the Meat button and cook for the default time of 35 minutes. When timer beeps, let pressure release naturally until float valve drops and then unlock lid. Serve warm.

Tailgating Chili

If you're looking to cook up some chili for game day, then this is the perfect recipe for you. If you'd like, use thinly sliced jalapeños to top off this hearty bowl of chili, spice up your day, and get you through the pregame jitters. Fire up your Instant Pot® and get ready to enjoy some tailgating with your friends.

- **Hands-On Time: 15 minutes**
- **Cook Time: 40 minutes**

Serves 6

1 tablespoon olive oil

1 pound beef stew cubes

1 medium onion, peeled and diced

4 cloves garlic, minced

½ cup beef broth

1 (16-ounce) can chili beans, including juice

2 cups sliced mushrooms

2 tablespoons chili powder

1 teaspoon red pepper flakes

1 tablespoon Italian seasoning

1 teaspoon sea salt

½ teaspoon ground black pepper

2 tablespoons tomato paste

1 (14.5-ounce) can diced tomatoes, including juice

1 Press the Sauté button on the Instant Pot®. Heat the oil and add the beef stew cubes and onion. Stir-fry for 3 minutes, searing beef and stir-frying until the onions are translucent. Add the garlic. Sauté for an additional 2 minutes.

2 Add beef broth to the Instant Pot® and deglaze by scraping any of the bits from the bottom and sides of the Instant Pot®. Stir in the remaining ingredients. Lock lid.

3 Press the Meat button and cook for the default time of 35 minutes. When timer beeps, let pressure release naturally until float valve drops and then unlock lid.

4 Ladle into individual bowls and serve warm.

INSTANT POT® OPTIONS

Let your guests garnish their chili with options such as sliced jalapeños, shredded cheese, sour cream, sliced black olives, and crushed tortilla chips.

Moroccan Lamb Stew

This stew is bursting with flavors and is served best with a side of couscous with a little dollop of plain yogurt on top. Before squeezing the orange for the juice, add the zest from the orange peel and a few sliced almonds to your couscous for a little zip.

- **Hands-On Time: 15 minutes**
- **Cook Time: 40 minutes**

Serves 6

2 tablespoons olive oil

2 pounds cubed boneless lamb

1 medium onion, peeled and diced

4 garlic cloves, minced

¼ cup freshly squeezed orange juice

2 cups beef broth

1 cup crushed tomatoes

¼ cup diced pitted dates

¼ cup diced dried apricots

2 teaspoons ground cumin

¼ teaspoon ground cinnamon

¼ teaspoon cayenne pepper

2 teaspoons minced fresh ginger

1 teaspoon sea salt

½ teaspoon ground black pepper

½ cup chopped fresh cilantro

1. Press the Sauté button on the Instant Pot®. Heat the oil and add the lamb cubes and onion. Stir-fry for 3–5 minutes, searing lamb and stir-frying until the onions are translucent. Add the garlic. Sauté for an additional minute.

2. Add orange juice and beef broth to the Instant Pot® and deglaze by scraping any of the bits from the side of the Instant Pot®. Stir in the remaining ingredients (except cilantro). Lock lid.

3. Press the Meat button and cook for the default time of 35 minutes. When timer beeps, let pressure release naturally until float valve drops and then unlock lid.

4. Ladle into individual bowls, garnish with cilantro, and serve warm.

Chicken and Mushroom Soup

This recipe takes simple, inexpensive ingredients and elevates them to a hearty, healthy meal that is worthy of a pricey restaurant. Serve a grilled cheese sandwich or a simple salad alongside this meal and you will have a happy household.

- **Hands-On Time: 15 minutes**
- **Cook Time: 25 minutes**

Serves 4

1 pound chicken thighs, cut in ½" cubes
1 teaspoon sea salt
½ teaspoon ground black pepper
2 tablespoons butter
1 small onion, peeled and diced
1 large carrot, peeled and diced
1 stalk celery, diced
2 cups sliced mushrooms
4 cups chicken broth
2 teaspoons dried thyme
1 teaspoon dried oregano
1 teaspoon garlic powder
¼ teaspoon cayenne pepper
½ cup heavy cream

1 Season the chicken with salt and pepper. Set aside.

2 Press the Sauté button on the Instant Pot® and heat the butter. Add the chicken, onion, carrot, celery, and mushrooms. Sauté for 3–5 minutes until the onions are translucent. Add the broth, thyme, oregano, garlic powder, and cayenne pepper. Lock lid.

3 Press the Soup button and adjust time to 20 minutes. When timer beeps, let pressure release naturally for 10 minutes. Quick-release any additional pressure until float valve drops and then unlock lid.

4 Stir in heavy cream. Ladle into bowls and serve warm.

INSTANT POT® OPTIONS
Mushrooms add a woody and unique flavor to many dishes. Each variety brings a slightly different flavor note. Oyster mushrooms have a brininess to them, shiitakes have a smokiness, and morels have a fabulous nuttiness. Change up the variety of mushroom that you use in this recipe or use a mix of varieties instead.

Split Pea Soup

Split pea soup has been consumed dating back to the Greeks and Romans and today is found in many regional cuisines. Each culture has its own variation. While this dish usually takes hours to prepare, the Instant Pot® will have these green split peas tender and in your mouth in no time. And don't skip the ham hock as it adds a saltiness that makes this dish irresistible.

- **Hands-On Time: 10 minutes**
- **Cook Time: 35 minutes**

Serves 4

1 tablespoon bacon grease

1 large sweet onion, peeled and diced

2 celery stalks, sliced

2 large carrots, peeled and diced

1½ cups dried green split peas, rinsed

5 cups chicken broth

1 teaspoon dried oregano

1 pound smoked ham hock

½ teaspoon sea salt

½ teaspoon ground black pepper

4 tablespoons sour cream

1 Press the Sauté button on the Instant Pot® and heat the bacon grease. Add the onion, celery, and carrots. Sauté for 3–5 minutes until the onions are translucent. Add peas, chicken broth, oregano, ham hock, salt, and pepper. Lock lid.

2 Press the Soup button and let cook for the default time of 30 minutes. When the timer beeps, quick-release pressure until float valve drops and then unlock lid.

3 Ladle into four bowls and garnish each with 1 tablespoon sour cream. Serve warm.

Heirloom Tomato Basil Soup

If you love tomato soup, this dish is going to make your day. And if you'd like to make this soup even better, top it with grilled-cheese croutons. Make a grilled-cheese sandwich as you normally would and then cut the sandwich into little squares. Float these glorious croutons atop your soup and enjoy this new twist on an old classic.

- **Hands-On Time: 10 minutes**
- **Cook Time: 15 minutes**

Serves 4

1 tablespoon olive oil

1 small onion, peeled and diced

1 celery stalk, sliced

8 medium heirloom tomatoes, seeded and quartered

¼ cup julienned fresh basil

1 teaspoon sea salt

3 cups chicken broth

1 cup heavy cream

1 teaspoon ground black pepper

1　Press the Sauté button on the Instant Pot® and heat the oil. Add the onion and celery and sauté for 3–5 minutes until the onions are translucent. Add the tomatoes. Continue to sauté for 3 minutes until tomatoes are tender and start to break down. Add basil, salt, and broth. Lock lid.

2　Press the Manual button and adjust time to 7 minutes. When timer beeps, quick-release pressure until float valve drops and then unlock lid.

3　Add heavy cream and pepper. In the Instant Pot®, purée soup with an immersion blender, or use a stand blender and purée in batches. Ladle into bowls and serve warm.

Thai Coconut Carrot Soup

PALEO, GLUTEN-FREE

Sweet and spicy, crunchy and smooth, this dish has a little bit of everything. It brings every side of your tongue alive while lulling you into a dream state. Try this dish with some diced chicken or shrimp or serve with some crusty bread for a crunch!

- **Hands-On Time: 15 minutes**
- **Cook Time: 25 minutes**

Serves 6

1 tablespoon coconut oil

1 small onion, peeled and diced

1 pound carrots, peeled and diced

2 cloves garlic, minced

1 tablespoon Thai red curry paste

4 cups vegetable broth

1 teaspoon honey

1 cup canned coconut milk

1 tablespoon fresh lime juice

¼ teaspoon red pepper flakes

1 teaspoon sea salt

½ teaspoon ground black pepper

¼ cup julienned fresh basil, plus 3 tablespoons for garnish

1 Press the Sauté button on the Instant Pot® and heat the coconut oil. Add the onion and carrots. Sauté for 3–5 minutes until onions are translucent. Add the garlic and curry paste. Continue to sauté for 1 minute. Add remaining ingredients, except 3 tablespoons basil. Lock lid.

2 Press the Soup button and adjust time to 20 minutes. When timer beeps, let pressure release naturally for 10 minutes. Quick-release any additional pressure until float valve drops and then unlock lid.

3 In the Instant Pot®, purée soup with an immersion blender, or use a stand blender and purée in batches.

4 Ladle into bowls, garnish each bowl with ½ tablespoon basil, and serve warm.

Savory Butternut Squash Soup

PALEO, GLUTEN-FREE

The addition of hot sauce and onion gives this traditionally sweet soup a bit of a savory edge. Creamy and healthy, this recipe will be sure to warm your heart and fill your belly on a chilly autumn night.

- **Hands-On Time: 15 minutes**
- **Cook Time: 25 minutes**

Serves 6

1 tablespoon olive oil

1 small onion, peeled and diced

2 celery stalks, sliced

3 pounds butternut squash, peeled, seeded, and cubed

1 small Granny Smith apple, peeled, cored, and diced

1 teaspoon sea salt

¼ teaspoon white pepper

1 teaspoon celery seed

¼ teaspoon ground nutmeg

¼ teaspoon hot sauce

1" piece of fresh ginger, peeled and minced

4 cups chicken broth

1 Press the Sauté button on the Instant Pot® and heat the oil. Add the onion and celery. Sauté for 5 minutes until onions are translucent. Add the butternut squash and apple. Continue to sauté for 2–3 minutes until apples are tender. Add remaining ingredients. Lock lid.

2 Press the Manual button and adjust time to 15 minutes. When timer beeps, quick-release pressure until float valve drops and then unlock lid.

3 In the Instant Pot®, purée soup with an immersion blender, or use a stand blender and purée in batches. Ladle into bowls and serve warm.

Butternut Squash Seed Garnish

Don't throw away those butternut squash seeds! They are the perfect garnish for this soup. Toss the cleaned seeds with 1 teaspoon of hot sauce and 1 teaspoon of fine sea salt and bake them at 200°F for approximately 30 minutes, flipping once. Garnish soup with seeds before serving and enjoy!

Summer Corn Chowder

Although you can use frozen or canned corn in this recipe, if you can get your hands on some fresh corn, take the extra time to cut the kernels from the cob. The difference in taste is night and day. Also, if you can pick your corn up from a roadside stand or farmers' market, it's even better because you are supporting your local farmers.

- **Hands-On Time: 20 minutes**
- **Cook Time: 25 minutes**

Serves 8

6 slices bacon, divided

1 large sweet onion, peeled and diced

1 large carrot, peeled and diced

½ cup diced celery

2 large Yukon gold potatoes, peeled and diced small

6 cups chicken broth

1 bay leaf

1 teaspoon sea salt

1 teaspoon ground black pepper

3 cups (about 5 medium ears of corn) fresh corn kernels

2 tablespoons fresh thyme leaves, divided

½ teaspoon honey

1 cup heavy cream

1 Press the Sauté button on the Instant Pot® and fry the bacon. Remove from the Instant Pot® and set aside on a paper-towel-lined plate. Add the onion, carrot, and celery. Sauté for 3–5 minutes until the onions are translucent. Add the potatoes. Continue to sauté for 2–3 minutes until potatoes start to brown. Add broth, bay leaf, salt, pepper, corn, 1 tablespoon thyme, and honey. Crumble 2 pieces of the bacon and add to the soup. Lock lid.

2 Press the Manual button and adjust time to 15 minutes. When timer beeps, quick-release pressure until float valve drops and then unlock lid.

3 Discard bay leaf. Add heavy cream and purée the soup in the Instant Pot® with an immersion blender, or use a stand blender and purée in batches.

4 Ladle into bowls and garnish with remaining 1 tablespoon thyme leaves and crumbled remaining bacon. Serve warm.

Broccoli Cheddar Soup

This soup is such an easy way to get some of your picky eaters to eat their broccoli, and it's so delicious that it just flies out of the pot. Thank goodness the Instant Pot® can make this Broccoli Cheddar Soup in minutes, because your family and guests will be screaming for seconds—and maybe thirds!

- **Hands-On Time: 10 minutes**
- **Cook Time: 25 minutes**

Serves 4

2 tablespoons butter

1 medium sweet onion, peeled and chopped

1 large carrot, peeled and chopped

2 cloves garlic, chopped

1 large bunch broccoli, coarsely chopped

½ cup chardonnay

3 cups chicken broth

1 teaspoon sea salt

½ teaspoon ground black pepper

Pinch of ground nutmeg

½ cup whole milk

1 cup sharp Cheddar cheese

1 Press the Sauté button on the Instant Pot® and heat the butter. Add onion, carrot, and garlic. Sauté for 5 minutes until the onions are translucent. Add the broccoli. Continue to sauté for 3 minutes until broccoli starts to become tender. Add wine, broth, salt, pepper, and nutmeg. Press the Adjust button to change the temperature to Less and simmer for 5 minutes. Lock lid.

2 Press the Manual button and adjust time to 10 minutes. When timer beeps, quick-release pressure until float valve drops and then unlock lid.

3 Add milk and cheese. In the Instant Pot®, purée the soup with an immersion blender, or use a stand blender and purée in batches.

4 Ladle into bowls and serve warm.

Cabbage and Smoked Sausage Soup

If you're looking for a quick Oktoberfest meal, you've found it. This tasty soup has all of the staples of a German meal: sausage, cabbage, beer, mustard, potatoes, and heartiness. Nothing soothes the soul better than this warm bowl of soup.

- **Hands-On Time: 15 minutes**
- **Cook Time: 35 minutes**

Serves 4

1 tablespoon olive oil

1 small onion, peeled and diced

1 large carrot, peeled and diced

1 stalk celery, diced

1 small Russet potato, peeled and diced small

1 pound smoked sausage, sliced

1 cup lager

3 cups chicken broth

1 tablespoon whole-grain mustard

1 (28-ounce) can diced tomatoes, including juice

1 small head cabbage, cored and thin chopped

½ teaspoon caraway seeds

½ teaspoon sea salt

½ teaspoon ground black pepper

1 Press the Sauté button on the Instant Pot® and heat the olive oil. Add the onion, carrot, and celery. Sauté for 3–5 minutes until onions are translucent. Add potatoes and sausage. Continue to stir-fry for an additional 3 minutes until potatoes start to brown.

2 Add lager to the Instant Pot® and deglaze by scraping the brown bits from the edges of the Instant Pot®. Press the Adjust button to change the temperature to Less and simmer unlidded for 5 minutes. Add broth, mustard, tomatoes, cabbage, caraway seeds, salt, and pepper. Lock lid.

3 Press the Soup button and adjust the time for 20 minutes. When timer beeps, let pressure release naturally for 10 minutes. Quick-release any additional pressure until float valve drops and then unlock lid.

4 Ladle into bowls and serve warm.

Creole Gumbo

This out-of-this-world Creole Gumbo will bring a bit of spice to your night, and if you close your eyes, it will make you think you're eating out at one of New Orleans's local restaurants. That's how authentic this gumbo is. So plug in your Instant Pot® and get your taste buds ready to take a quick vacation down South.

- **Hands-On Time: 15 minutes**
- **Cook Time: 30 minutes**

Serves 4

1 tablespoon bacon grease

1 medium onion, peeled and diced

2 stalks celery, diced

1 small red bell pepper, seeded and diced

½ pound chicken thighs, ½" diced

1 pound andouille sausage, sliced

3 cloves garlic, minced

3 cups chicken broth

1 teaspoon Worcestershire sauce

¼ cup flour

1 pound medium shrimp, peeled, deveined, tails removed

1 tablespoon filé powder

1 teaspoon garlic powder

1 teaspoon cayenne pepper

1 teaspoon fresh thyme leaves

¼ cup chopped fresh parsley, divided

10 ounces frozen or fresh sliced okra

1 (14.5-ounce) can stewed tomatoes, including juice

2 cups cooked rice

1 Press the Sauté button on the Instant Pot® and heat the bacon grease. Add the onion, celery, and bell pepper. Sauté for 3–5 minutes until the onions are translucent. Add chicken, sausage, and garlic. Continue to stir-fry for an additional 2–3 minutes until chicken is no longer pink.

2 Add chicken broth and deglaze the Instant Pot® by scraping the brown bits from the bottom and sides of the Instant Pot®. Add Worcestershire sauce, flour, shrimp, filé powder, garlic powder, cayenne pepper, thyme, ⅛ cup parsley, okra, and stewed tomatoes. Lock lid.

3 Press the Soup button and adjust time to 20 minutes. When timer beeps, let pressure release naturally for 10 minutes. Quick-release any additional pressure until float valve drops and then unlock lid.

4 Ladle into bowls and serve warm over a scoop of rice; garnish with remaining ⅛ cup chopped parsley.

Loaded Potato Soup

This Loaded Potato Soup is stick-to-your ribs tasty on its own, but it's even more so when you top it with garnishes that you let your guests personalize. Set out a garnish station so your guests can load their potato soup with their favorite toppings chosen from crumbled bacon, shredded sharp Cheddar cheese, chopped green onions, or a dollop of sour cream.

- **Hands-On Time: 10 minutes**
- **Cook Time: 30 minutes**

Serves 4

2 slices bacon, diced
4 tablespoons butter
1 medium sweet onion, peeled and chopped
1 large carrot, peeled and diced
2 cloves garlic, chopped
4 cups peeled and diced potatoes
4 cups chicken broth
1 teaspoon sea salt
1 teaspoon ground black pepper
Pinch of ground nutmeg
1 cup whole milk

1 Press the Sauté button on the Instant Pot® and stir-fry the bacon until almost crisp. Add the butter, onion, and carrot. Sauté for 3–5 minutes until the onions are translucent. Add garlic and sauté for an additional minute. Add potatoes. Continue to sauté for 2–3 minutes until potatoes are browned. Add in broth, salt, pepper, and nutmeg. Lock lid.

2 Press the Soup button and adjust the time for 20 minutes. When timer beeps, quick-release pressure until float valve drops and then unlock lid.

3 Add the milk. In the Instant Pot®, purée the soup with an immersion blender, or use a stand blender and purée in batches. Ladle into bowls and serve warm.

Hearty Minestrone Soup

This classic Italian soup is loaded with vegetables and robust Mediterranean flavors. Also included is orzo, a rice-shaped pasta, which adds to the heartiness of this scrumptious soup.

- **Hands-On Time: 10 minutes**
- **Cook Time: 30 minutes**

Serves 4

2 cups dried Great Northern beans

1 cup orzo

2 large carrots, peeled and diced

1 bunch Swiss chard, ribs removed and roughly chopped

1 medium zucchini, diced

2 stalks celery, diced

1 medium onion, peeled and diced

1 teaspoon minced garlic

1 tablespoon Italian seasoning

1 teaspoon salt

½ teaspoon ground black pepper

2 bay leaves

1 (14.5-ounce) can diced tomatoes, including juice

4 cups vegetable broth

1 cup tomato juice

4 sprigs fresh parsley for garnish

1 Rinse beans and add to the Instant Pot® with remaining ingredients except parsley. Lock the lid.

2 Press the Soup button and cook for the default time of 30 minutes. When timer beeps, let pressure release naturally for 10 minutes.

3 Quick-release any additional pressure until float valve drops and then unlock lid. Ladle into bowls, garnish each bowl with a sprig of parsley, and serve warm.

Beans, Rice, and Grains

Tired of soaking your dried beans overnight? Tired of eating highly processed rice and grains so that they will cook quicker? Fortunately, your Instant Pot® can solve these problems and you'll be eating rice and beans in no time. Be sure to carefully follow the recipe instructions in this chapter as the beans, rice, and grains continue to cook in the steam during the natural-release phase of Instant Pot® cooking. If you release the pressure too early, it could result in inedible little pebbles. Plus, starchy items can clog up the anti-block shield if the pressure is released too quickly. So plug in your Instant Pot® and get ready to enjoy recipes such as Wild Rice with Hazelnuts and Dried Apricots, Rotini with Mushroom Cream Sauce, Black Bean Sliders, and more.

Simple Jasmine Rice

Fragrant and floral, jasmine rice is best served alongside Asian dishes. This is also an excellent choice to serve with Creole Gumbo (see recipe in Chapter 3) or even as a simple side dish with most meat dishes.

- **Hands-On Time: 2 minutes**
- **Cook Time: 3 minutes**

Serves 4

2 cups jasmine rice
1¼ cups water
1 cup chicken broth
1 teaspoon sea salt
1 tablespoon butter

1 Place all ingredients into the Instant Pot®.

2 Press the Manual button and manually set the time to 3 minutes. When the timer beeps, unplug the Instant Pot® and let the pressure release naturally until float valve drops and then unlock lid. Serve.

Easy Couscous

If you're a *Pineapple Express* fan, you know that couscous is the "food so nice they named it twice." Couscous, the national dish of Morocco, is small granules of pasta made from semolina flour. Traditionally, they are actually rolled out by hand and are then set out to dry. Serve this recipe as a side dish or add some meat and vegetables during the cooking process for a more complete meal.

- **Hands-On Time: 5 minutes**
- **Cook Time: 4 minutes**

Serves 6

2 cups couscous
2½ cups water
1 cup chicken broth
1 teaspoon sea salt
1 tablespoon butter
1 teaspoon lemon zest

1 Place all ingredients into the Instant Pot®. Lock lid.

2 Press the Manual button and adjust time to 4 minutes. When timer beeps, let pressure release naturally until float valve drops and then unlock lid. Serve.

Simple Israeli Couscous

Also known as "pearl couscous," Israeli couscous is larger than the traditional grain. Chewier and nutty in flavor, the mouthfeel is closely related to barley. Blend with a combination of spices and herbs to accompany almost any main dish.

- **Hands-On Time: 5 minutes**
- **Cook Time: 10 minutes**

Serves 4

1 tablespoon sesame oil
2 small shallots, minced
1 cup pearl couscous
2 cups vegetable broth
1 teaspoon sea salt
1 teaspoon lemon zest

1 Press the Sauté button on the Instant Pot®. Heat oil. Add shallots and couscous. Stir-fry for 3–4 minutes until browned. Add broth. Lock lid.

2 Press the Manual button and adjust time to 5 minutes. When timer beeps, let pressure release naturally for 5 minutes. Quick-release any additional pressure until float valve drops and then unlock lid.

3 Drain liquid. Stir in salt and lemon zest. Serve.

Down South Savory Porridge

Congee, jook, bubur, rice porridge . . . whatever you call this dish, it is all good. This recipe takes porridge down South and gives it an unconventional twist. Serve this porridge with biscuits or cornmeal muffins on the side to sop up all of its goodness!

- **Hands-On Time: 5 minutes**
- **Cook Time: 25 minutes**

Serves 4

1 tablespoon bacon grease
1 large Vidalia onion, peeled and diced
1 cup sliced cooked sausage
1 cup jasmine rice
1 cup water
1 cup vegetable broth
1 cup shredded Cheddar cheese

1 Press the Sauté button on the Instant Pot® and heat bacon grease. Add onion and sausage and cook 3–5 minutes until onions are translucent.

2 Add a level layer of rice. Slowly pour in water and broth. Lock lid.

3 Press the Porridge button and cook for the default time of 20 minutes. When timer beeps, let pressure release naturally for 10 minutes. Quick-release any additional pressure until float valve drops and then unlock lid.

Red Beans and Chorizo

This spicy dish feels right at home when spooned over rice. Add some julienned radishes for some crunch and texture, and spice things up by serving this dish with your favorite hot sauce on the side.

- **Hands-On Time: 15 minutes**
- **Cook Time: 35 minutes**

Serves 8

1 cup dried red beans

1 tablespoon olive oil

1 small onion, peeled and diced

1 small green bell pepper, seeded and diced

2 stalks celery, diced

½ pound chorizo, loose or removed from casing

3 cups chicken broth

1 (14.5-ounce) can diced tomatoes, including juice

½ teaspoon garlic powder

½ teaspoon ground cumin

½ teaspoon garlic powder

½ teaspoon sea salt

2 teaspoons Creole seasoning

1 cup shredded Cheddar cheese

1 Rinse and drain beans.

2 Press the Sauté button on Instant Pot® and heat olive oil. Add onion, bell pepper, celery, and chorizo. Stir-fry 3–5 minutes until onions are translucent. Add broth and deglaze the Instant Pot® by scraping the sides and bottom of the Instant Pot®.

3 Add beans and remaining ingredients. Lock lid.

4 Press the Bean button and cook for the default time of 30 minutes. When timer beeps, let pressure release naturally for 10 minutes. Quick-release any additional pressure until float valve drops and then unlock lid.

5 Using a slotted spoon, transfer beans to a serving bowl. Let cool to thicken and serve.

6 Stir in Cheddar cheese and transfer to four bowls. Serve warm.

Wild Rice with Hazelnuts and Dried Apricots

If the autumn leaves are turning colors and the air is crisp, you know this dish is about to become a favorite on your fall table. This soothing recipe, along with a crisp glass of char-donnay, is the perfect end to a perfect day spent apple picking, pumpkin picking, or more. Feel free to garnish with snipped chives to take this dish up a notch and impress your guests.

- **Hands-On Time: 5 minutes**
- **Cook Time: 30 minutes**

Serves 8

2 cups wild rice, rinsed
3 cups vegetable broth
2½ cups water
2 teaspoons sea salt
1 tablespoon butter
½ cup chopped hazelnuts
½ cup chopped dried
    apricots

1 Place all ingredients into Instant Pot®. Lock lid.

2 Press the Manual button and adjust time to 30 minutes. When timer beeps, let pressure release naturally for 5 minutes. Quick-release any additional pressure until float valve drops and then unlock lid.

3 Transfer to a dish and serve warm.

Parmesan Risotto

There are many amazing things about an Instant Pot®, and one of them is this delicious Parmesan Risotto. No longer do you have to stand over a skillet stirring constantly. Now you can get dinner on the table and get done whatever it is that you need to get done, all without breaking a sweat.

- **Hands-On Time: 5 minutes**
- **Cook Time: 20 minutes**

Serves 4

4 tablespoons butter

1 small onion, peeled and finely diced

2 cloves garlic, minced

1½ cups Arborio rice

4 cups chicken broth, divided

3 tablespoons grated Parmesan cheese

½ teaspoon salt

¼ teaspoon ground black pepper

½ cup chopped fresh parsley

1 Press the Sauté button on Instant Pot®. Add and melt the butter. Add the onion and stir-fry for 3–5 minutes until onions are translucent. Add garlic and rice and cook for an additional minute. Add 1 cup broth and stir for 2–3 minutes until it is absorbed by the rice.

2 Add remaining 3 cups broth, Parmesan cheese, salt, and pepper. Lock lid.

3 Press the Manual button and adjust time to 10 minutes. When timer beeps, let pressure release naturally for 10 minutes. Quick-release any additional pressure until float valve drops and then unlock lid.

4 Ladle into bowls and garnish each with ⅛ cup fresh parsley.

What Is Arborio Rice?

Arborio rice is a short-grained, starchy rice that lends itself so well to those creamy risotto dishes. Named for the city it was originally grown in, Arborio rice blends well with a multitude of flavors. Not only do savory dishes work well with this variety, but Arborio rice is also a great choice for rice pudding.

Spinach-Feta Risotto

Let this mash-up of two countries, Greece and Italy, marry together in this incredibly creamy, tasty dish. The brininess of the kalamata olives is the perfect finishing touch to this savory recipe.

- **Hands-On Time: 5 minutes**
- **Cook Time: 20 minutes**

Serves 4

3 tablespoons olive oil

1 small onion, peeled and finely diced

2 cloves garlic, minced

1½ cups Arborio rice

4 cups chicken broth, divided

3 tablespoons grated Parmesan cheese

½ teaspoon salt

¼ teaspoon ground black pepper

½ cup julienned spinach

¼ cup crumbled feta cheese

¼ cup pitted and finely diced kalamata olives

1 Press the Sauté button on the Instant Pot® and heat the oil. Add the onion and stir-fry for 3–5 minutes until onions are translucent. Add garlic and rice and cook for an additional 1 minute. Add 1 cup broth and stir for 2–3 minutes until it is absorbed by the rice.

2 Add remaining 3 cups broth, Parmesan cheese, salt, and pepper. Lock lid.

3 Press the Manual button and cook for 10 minutes. When timer beeps, let pressure release naturally for 10 minutes. Quick-release any additional pressure until float valve drops and then unlock lid.

4 Stir in spinach and feta cheese. Transfer a to serving dish and garnish with kalamata olives.

Millet Tabouleh

Traditionally made with bulgur, this twist on a traditional tabouleh can easily be served as a vegetarian main dish with grape leaves, enjoyed as a chilled lunch salad bowl, or accompany a main meal as a side dish. The choice is up to you!

- **Hands-On Time: 15 minutes**
- **Cook Time: 10 minutes**

Serves 4

1½ cups chopped fresh parsley

¼ cup chopped fresh mint leaves

1 cup peeled and diced red onion

¼ cup small-diced zucchini

½ cup peeled, seeded, and small-diced cucumber

4 small Roma tomatoes, seeded and diced

¼ cup plus 2 teaspoons olive oil, divided

¼ cup lemon juice

1 teaspoon lemon zest

1½ teaspoons sea salt, divided

¼ teaspoon ground black pepper

1 cup millet

2 cups vegetable broth

1 In a medium bowl, combine parsley, mint, onion, zucchini, cucumber, tomatoes, ¼ cup olive oil, lemon juice, lemon zest, 1 teaspoon salt, and pepper. Cover and refrigerate for 30 minutes up to overnight.

2 Drizzle 2 teaspoons olive oil in Instant Pot®. Add millet to Instant Pot® in an even layer. Add broth and remaining ½ teaspoon salt. Lock lid.

3 Press the Rice button (the Instant Pot® will determine the cooking time, about 10 minutes pressurized cooking time). When the timer beeps, let pressure release naturally for 5 minutes. Quick-release any additional pressure until float valve drops and then unlock lid.

4 Transfer millet to a serving bowl and set aside to cool. When cooled, add to refrigerated mixture and stir. Serve.

Spanish Rice

The saffron threads add a smoky, slightly floral note to this dish. The flavor is hard to describe and has been argued about by many chefs over the years. Serve this as a side dish or add some shrimp, mussels, peas, and parsley for a quick paella.

- **Hands-On Time: 10 minutes**
- **Cook Time: 15 minutes**

Serves 6

1 tablespoon olive oil

1 medium onion, peeled and diced

1 medium yellow bell pepper, seeded and diced small

3 cloves garlic, minced

1 cup basmati rice

1 cup chicken broth

1 (14.5-ounce) can diced tomatoes, including juice

1 small jalapeño pepper, seeded and diced

¼ teaspoon saffron threads

½ teaspoon ground cumin

⅛ teaspoon cayenne pepper

1 teaspoon sea salt

½ teaspoon ground black pepper

1 Press the Sauté button on Instant Pot®. Heat olive oil and add onion and bell pepper. Stir-fry for 3–5 minutes until onions are translucent. Add garlic. Cook for an additional minute. Add basmati rice and toss to combine. Add chicken broth to the Instant Pot® and deglaze by scraping the bottom and sides of the Instant Pot®.

2 Add remaining ingredients to Instant Pot®. Lock lid.

3 Press the Rice button (the Instant Pot® will determine the cooking time; 1 cup rice takes about 10 minutes pressurized cooking time). When the timer beeps, let pressure release naturally for 10 minutes. Quick-release any additional pressure until float valve drops and then unlock lid.

4 Transfer to a dish and serve warm.

What Are Saffron Threads?

Known as the world's most expensive spice, saffron can be purchased ground or in threads. They are the yellow stigma found on the purple crocus, with only three on each flower. The elevated price comes from the fact that they are hand-picked and dried, which results in a highly labor-intensive process.

Creamy Chicken and Broccoli over Rice

The Italian-seasoned coating on this chicken not only allows the chicken to be flavorful, but some of the flour will fall off during the cooking process and will work to thicken the cream, giving it a luxurious, creamy mouthfeel.

- **Hands-On Time: 15 minutes**
- **Cook Time: 45 minutes**

Serves 8

¼ cup flour
2 teaspoons salt
½ teaspoon ground black pepper
1 tablespoon Italian seasoning
1 pound chicken thighs, cut in 1" chunks
1 tablespoon olive oil
1 large onion, peeled and diced
2 cups wild rice, rinsed
3 cups vegetable broth
1½ cups water
2 cups steamed broccoli florets
¼ cup heavy cream
¼ cup grated Parmesan cheese

1   In a small bowl, combine flour, salt, pepper, and Italian seasoning. Add chicken to seasoning mix and toss to coat. Set aside.

2   Press the Sauté button on the Instant Pot® and heat oil. Cook onions for 3–5 minutes until translucent. Add rice and toss to combine.

3   Add chicken in an even layer over ingredients in Instant Pot®. Gently pour in broth and water. Lock lid.

4   Press the Multigrain button (the Instant Pot® will determine the cooking time, but wild rice takes about 40 minutes pressurized cooking time). When the timer beeps, let pressure release naturally for 10 minutes. Quick-release any additional pressure until float valve drops and then unlock lid. Add broccoli. Stir. Add cream and Parmesan cheese. Stir. Allow mixture to thicken unlidded in Instant Pot® for 5 minutes.

5   Transfer to a serving dish and serve warm.

Lentil-Spinach Curry

There are so many reasons to make this vegetarian dish! It is quick, full of nutrients, and fragrant from the mix of spices! Alter this recipe by utilizing the rich greens depending on the season by subbing out the spinach for chard, kale, collards, and even beet greens.

- **Hands-On Time: 5 minutes**
- **Cook Time: 12 minutes**

Serves 4

1 tablespoon olive oil

½ cup peeled and diced onion

1 clove garlic, minced

1 cup yellow lentils

4 cups water

½ teaspoon ground coriander

½ teaspoon ground turmeric

½ teaspoon curry powder

½ cup diced tomato

2 cups fresh spinach

1 Press the Sauté button on Instant Pot®. Heat olive oil and add onions. Stir-fry 3–5 minutes until onions are translucent. Add garlic and cook for an additional minute. Add lentils and toss to combine. Pour in water. Lock lid.

2 Press the Manual button and adjust time to 6 minutes. When the timer beeps, quick-release the pressure until float valve drops and then unlock lid. Drain any residual liquid. Toss in coriander, turmeric, and curry powder. Stir in tomato and fresh spinach.

3 Press Sauté button on the Instant Pot®, press Adjust button to change the heat to Less, and simmer unlidded until tomatoes are heated through and spinach has wilted.

4 Transfer to a dish and serve.

Black Bean Sliders

In addition to how quick and easy these Black Bean Sliders are to make, the way you can personalize this dish really makes this recipe a keeper. Top these spiced Black Bean Sliders with fresh slices of avocado, tomato, and red onion. Then add a little kick with some chipotle mayonnaise. Whatever you want to add, do it! Your mouth will thank you.

- **Hands-On Time: 10 minutes**
- **Cook Time: 50 minutes**

Serves 8

1 cup dried black beans
1 tablespoon olive oil
1 slice bacon
1 small red bell pepper,
    seeded and diced small
2 cups vegetable broth
½ teaspoon garlic powder
¼ teaspoon coriander
½ teaspoon chili powder
½ teaspoon ground cumin
½ teaspoon sea salt
¼ cup chopped fresh cilantro
1 large egg
1 cup panko bread crumbs
16 slider buns

INSTANT POT® OPTIONS

If you want to spice up your Black Bean Sliders, just add a dollop of this Quick Chipotle Mayonnaise. In a small food processor, pulse together 1 cup mayonnaise, ¼ cup sour cream, 2 chipotles in adobo sauce, 1 tablespoon lime juice, and a pinch or two of salt. Refrigerate overnight until ready to serve.

1 Rinse and drain beans.

2 Press the Sauté button on Instant Pot® and heat olive oil. Add bacon and bell pepper. Stir-fry 3–5 minutes until bacon is cooked. Add broth and deglaze the Instant Pot® by scraping the sides and bottom of the Instant Pot®.

3 Add beans, garlic powder, coriander, chili powder, cumin, salt, and cilantro. Lock lid.

4 Press the Bean button and cook for the default time of 30 minutes. When timer beeps, let pressure release naturally for 10 minutes. Quick-release any additional pressure until float valve drops and then unlock lid.

5 Discard bacon. Press the Sauté button on the Instant Pot®, press the Adjust button to change the heat to Less, and simmer bean mixture unlidded for 10 minutes to thicken. Remove mixture to a large bowl. Once cool enough to handle, quickly mix in egg and bread crumbs.

6 Form into 16 equal-sized small patties. Cook on stovetop in a skillet for approximately 2–3 minutes per side until browned.

7 Remove from heat and add each patty to a bun. Serve warm.

Hoppin' John

This is traditionally a lucky dish served at New Year's in the South. The peas represent coins. To double up on your upcoming financial prosperity, add some Lucky Collard Greens (see recipe in Chapter 6). Put a scoop of each in your bowl and enjoy them together.

- **Hands-On Time: 5 minutes**
- **Cook Time: 35 minutes**

Serves 8

2 tablespoons olive oil, divided

1 large sweet onion, peeled and diced

1 small jalapeño, seeded and diced

2 stalks celery, diced small

3 cloves garlic, minced

2 cups dried black-eyed peas

1 cup basmati rice

2 cups chicken broth

3 cups water

1 ham hock

1 Press the Sauté button on the Instant Pot® and heat 1 tablespoon olive oil. Add onion, jalapeño, and celery and stir-fry 3–5 minutes until onions are translucent. Add garlic and heat for an additional 1 minute. Add remaining 1 tablespoon olive oil. Add black-eyed peas and toss to combine.

2 Add an even layer of rice. Slowly pour in broth and water. Add ham hock. Lock lid.

3 Press the Manual button and adjust time to 30 minutes. When the timer beeps, let pressure release naturally for 5 minutes. Quick-release any additional pressure until float valve drops and then unlock lid.

4 Dice meat off of the ham hock and discard bone. Stir ham into the rice mixture. Using a slotted spoon, transfer ingredients from the Instant Pot® to a bowl and serve warm.

Boston Baked Beans

The rich molasses flavor is what give these beans an edge. Show up to the BBQ with these sweet and tangy baked beans and watch the smiles grow. Great with burgers and dogs, this American side dish is a staple for all outdoor festivities.

- **Hands-On Time: 10 minutes**
- **Cook Time: 45 minutes**

Serves 10

1 tablespoon olive oil

5 slices bacon, diced

1 large sweet onion, peeled and diced

4 cloves garlic, minced

2 cups dried navy beans

4 cups chicken broth

2 teaspoons ground mustard

1 teaspoon sea salt

¼ teaspoon ground black pepper

¼ cup molasses

½ cup ketchup

¼ cup packed dark brown sugar

1 teaspoon smoked paprika

1 teaspoon Worcestershire sauce

1 teaspoon apple cider vinegar

1 Press Sauté button on Instant Pot®. Heat olive oil. Add bacon and onions. Stir-fry for 3–5 minutes until onions are translucent. Add garlic. Cook for an additional minute. Add beans. Toss to combine.

2 Add broth, mustard, salt, and pepper. Lock lid.

3 Press the Bean button and cook for the default time of 30 minutes. When timer beeps, let pressure release naturally for 10 minutes. Quick-release any additional pressure until float valve drops and then unlock lid.

4 Stir in the molasses, ketchup, brown sugar, smoked paprika, Worcestershire sauce, and vinegar. Press the Sauté button on the Instant Pot®, press the Adjust button to change the heat to Less, and simmer uncovered for 10 minutes to thicken the sauce; then transfer to a serving dish and serve warm.

Rotini with Mushroom Cream Sauce

Rotini is the perfect pasta for this mushroom sauce because the grooves catch all of the sauce's creaminess. Couple this with the saltiness of the bacon and the woodiness of the mushrooms and you have the perfect combination of a quick and tasty meal, elevated.

- **Hands-On Time: 5 minutes**
- **Cook Time: 15 minutes**

Serves 6

1 tablespoon olive oil
2 slices bacon, cubed
1 small onion, peeled and diced
3 cloves garlic, minced
1 pound rotini pasta
2 cups sliced white mushrooms
2 tablespoons flour
½ cup whole milk
1 teaspoon sea salt
½ teaspoon ground black pepper
1 tablespoon dried thyme
¼ cup grated Parmesan cheese
2 tablespoons butter

1　Press the Sauté button on the Instant Pot® and heat olive oil. Add bacon and onion and stir-fry for 3–5 minutes until onions are translucent. Add garlic and cook for an additional minute.

2　Place rotini in an even layer in Instant Pot®. Pour enough water to come about ¼" over pasta. Add a layer of mushrooms. Lock lid.

3　Press the Manual button and adjust time to 4 minutes. When the timer beeps, let pressure release naturally for 3 minutes. Quick-release any additional pressure until float valve drops and then unlock lid. Drain any residual water.

4　While pasta is cooking, in a small bowl whisk together flour, milk, salt, pepper, thyme, and Parmesan cheese to create a slurry. Set aside.

5　Pour slurry over pasta and stir. Add butter. Press Sauté button on the Instant Pot®, press Adjust button to change temperature to Less, and simmer unlidded for a few minutes to thicken the sauce. Stir and transfer to a dish and serve warm.

5

Appetizers

Appetizers are a great way to bring a group of people together to enjoy a game or hold them over until you serve a meal. But you don't want to have to wear your chef hat all day, stuck in the kitchen, so let the Instant Pot® be your helpful little sous chef. Quick, warm food in minutes? Now that's how you throw a party! With amazing appetizers ranging from Carne Asada Nachos and Crab and Artichoke Dip to Sticky Honey Chicken Wings and Mini Potato Skins, the only problem you'll have incorporating the recipes in this chapter into your next social event will be deciding which one to bring.

Peanut Butter and Jelly Chicken Wings

Bring back memories of the school lunchroom with this classic combination of ingredients and flavors. Try different varieties of jelly for a change in flavor profile. Fig preserves around the holidays are always popular, or you can always add an Asian flair with some jalapeño jelly and seasonings!

- **Hands-On Time: 10 minutes**
- **Cook Time: 10 minutes**

Serves 6

½ cup creamy peanut butter
1 cup grape jelly
2 tablespoons apple cider vinegar
1 teaspoon hot sauce
¼ teaspoon sea salt
2 pounds chicken wings
1 cup chicken broth
¼ cup chopped fresh basil

1 In a large bowl, whisk together peanut butter, jelly, apple cider vinegar, hot sauce, and salt.

2 If you buy chicken wings that are connected, cut them at the joint to separate. Add wings to peanut butter mixture and toss. Refrigerate covered for 1 hour.

3 Add chicken broth to Instant Pot®. Insert a steamer basket. Add chicken wings. Stand up wings if desired so as to not overcrowd them on top of each other. Lock lid.

4 Press the Manual button and adjust time to 10 minutes. When timer beeps, let pressure release naturally for 5 minutes. Quick-release any additional pressure until the float valve drops and then unlock the lid. Garnish with chopped basil. Serve.

Sticky Honey Chicken Wings

PALEO, GLUTEN-FREE

Chicken wings have become a national treasure in America, just like apple pie and baseball. Pop open a beer (keep it gluten-free!) and sit back and relax. These wings will be yours within the half-hour.

- **Hands-On Time: 10 minutes**
- **Cook Time: 10 minutes**

Serves 6

¼ cup honey
¼ cup freshly squeezed orange juice
¼ cup coconut aminos
1 tablespoon apple cider vinegar
2 tablespoons sriracha
3 cloves garlic, minced
½ teaspoon ground black pepper
2 pounds chicken wings
1 teaspoon sea salt
1 cup chicken broth

1 In a large bowl, whisk together honey, orange juice, coconut aminos, apple cider vinegar, sriracha, garlic, and black pepper. Set aside.

2 If you buy chicken wings that are connected, cut them at the joint to separate. Season chicken with salt. Set aside.

3 Add chicken broth to Instant Pot®. Insert a steamer basket. Add chicken wings. Stand up wings if necessary so as to not over-crowd them on top of each other. Lock lid.

4 Press the Manual button and adjust time to 10 minutes. When timer beeps, let pressure release naturally for 5 minutes. Quick-release any additional pressure until float valve drops and then unlock lid.

5 Toss the chicken in the sauce mixture. Serve.

Coconut Aminos, Tamari, and Soy Sauce

These three ingredients can be subbed out equally in recipes for each other. Coconut aminos are soy-free and gluten-free and can generally be found in specialty stores or the organic section of the grocery store. Tamari is a gluten-free soy-sauce substitute and is a little easier to find as it generally is sold right next to the soy sauce. Tastewise, you really cannot tell a difference, especially used in recipes with other ingredients.

Lemon Garlic Chicken Wings

PALEO, GLUTEN-FREE

Juicy and crispy chicken wings don't have to be bad for you. These wings are free of gluten, processed sugars, and bottled chemical combinations. And the simple and fresh flavors of lemon and garlic combine in this dish to make these wings amazingly delicious.

- **Hands-On Time: 10 minutes**
- **Cook Time: 15 minutes**

Serves 6

⅓ cup olive oil
¼ cup fresh lemon juice
1 tablespoon lemon zest
4 garlic cloves, minced
¼ teaspoon sea salt
Pinch of cayenne pepper
2 pounds chicken wings
1 cup chicken broth
¼ cup chopped parsley

1 In a large bowl, whisk together olive oil, lemon juice, lemon zest, garlic, salt, and cayenne pepper.

2 If you buy chicken wings that are connected, cut them at the joint to separate. Add wings to lemon juice mixture and toss. Refrigerate covered for 1 hour.

3 Add chicken broth to Instant Pot®. Insert a steamer basket. Add chicken wings. Stand up wings if desired so as to not overcrowd them on top of each other. Lock lid.

4 Press the Manual button and adjust time to 10 minutes. When the timer beeps, let pressure release naturally for 5 minutes. Quick-release any additional pressure until the float valve drops and then unlock the lid.

5 Place wings on a parchment-paper-lined baking sheet. Broil for 3–5 minutes until browned. Transfer to a serving plate and garnish with chopped parsley.

Black Bean Dip

Anyone can buy a black bean dip, but nothing compares to this quick, homemade version. Top this with a dollop of sour cream and surround it with a sea of tortilla chips, and you will be the hit of the party.

- **Hands-On Time: 10 minutes**
- **Cook Time: 35 minutes**

Serves 12

1 cup dried black beans

1 tablespoon olive oil

2 slices bacon, finely diced

1 small onion, peeled and diced

3 cloves garlic, minced

1 cup chicken broth

1 (14.5-ounce) can diced tomatoes, including juice

1 small jalapeño, seeded and diced small

1 teaspoon ground cumin

½ teaspoon smoked paprika

1 tablespoon fresh lime juice

½ teaspoon dried oregano

¼ cup finely chopped fresh cilantro

¼ teaspoon sea salt

1 Rinse and drain beans.

2 Press the Sauté button on Instant Pot® and heat olive oil Add bacon and onion. Stir-fry 3–5 minutes until onions are translucent. Add garlic and sauté for an additional minute. Add broth and deglaze the Instant Pot® by scraping the dark bits from the sides and bottom of the Instant Pot®. Add beans and remaining ingredients. Lock lid.

3 Press the Bean button and cook for the default time of 30 minutes. When timer beeps, let pressure release naturally for 10 minutes. Quick-release any additional pressure until the float valve drops and then unlock lid.

4 Use an immersion blender to blend ingredients in the Instant Pot® until desired smoothness is achieved. Serve warm.

Texas Caviar Dip

Although this recipe is a great appetizer that can be served with tortilla chips, don't count it out for a great bean side dish. Substitute Texas Caviar Dip in recipes that call for salsa as an accompaniment. It will add a new flavor combo to a tried-and-true staple that you didn't even realize needed an overhaul.

- **Hands-On Time: 15 minutes**
- **Cook Time: 35 minutes**

Serves 10

2 tablespoons plus ¼ cup olive oil, divided

1 large sweet onion, peeled and diced

1 small jalapeño, seeded and diced

2 stalks celery, diced small

3 cloves garlic, minced

2 cups dried black-eyed peas

1 slice bacon

2 cups chicken broth

1 cup water

1 small green bell pepper, seeded and diced

4 small Roma tomatoes, diced (including dicing juice)

2 cups corn kernels

½ small red onion, peeled and diced

Juice of 1 lime

1 tablespoon red wine vinegar

¼ cup chopped fresh cilantro

1 Heat 1 tablespoon olive oil in Instant Pot®. Add onion, jalapeño, and celery and stir-fry for 3–5 minutes until onions are translucent. Add garlic and heat for an additional minute. Add another tablespoon of olive oil. Add black-eyed peas and bacon. Toss to combine, then slowly pour in broth and water. Lock lid.

2 Press the Manual button and adjust time to 30 minutes. When timer beeps, let the pressure naturally release for 5 minutes. Quick-release any additional pressure until float valve drops and then unlock lid. Discard bacon.

3 Using a slotted spoon, transfer bean mixture to a serving dish. Let cool. Add in bell pepper, tomatoes, corn, red onion, lime juice, vinegar, ¼ cup olive oil, and cilantro and toss to combine. Refrigerate overnight to marry flavors. Serve warmed or chilled.

Chickpea Hummus

This Egyptian dish is a blend of chickpeas, olive oil, lemon, and tahini, a paste made from toasted sesame seeds. Hummus is traditionally scooped up with pita bread, but in Western areas, tortilla chips and sliced veggies are more the norm.

- **Hands-On Time: 10 minutes**
- **Cook Time: 35 minutes**

Serves 10

1 cup dried chickpeas
3 tablespoons olive oil, divided
2 cups water
2 cups vegetable broth
¼ cup tahini
Juice of 1 lemon
1 teaspoon lemon zest
1 teaspoon salt
3 cloves garlic, minced
2 teaspoons smoked paprika

1 Rinse and drain chickpeas.

2 Press the Sauté button on Instant Pot®. Heat 1 tablespoon olive oil. Toss in chickpeas and sauté for 2 minutes. Add water and vegetable broth. Lock lid.

3 Press the Bean button and cook for the default time of 30 minutes. When timer beeps, let pressure release naturally for 10 minutes. Quick-release any additional pressure until the float valve drops and then unlock lid.

4 Using a slotted spoon, transfer pot ingredients to a food processor or blender. Pulse. Add tahini, lemon juice, lemon zest, salt, and garlic. Add some of the cooking liquid from the Instant Pot® if hummus is too thick.

5 Transfer to a serving bowl and garnish with smoked paprika and remaining 2 tablespoons olive oil.

Classic Baba Ghanoush

This Mediterranean classic is a healthy alternative to the mayonnaise-based dips that you will frequently find at parties. Serve this with pita chips, crudités, or crostini and make your guests happy!

- **Hands-On Time: 10 minutes**
- **Cook Time: 10 minutes**

Makes 1½ cups

1 tablespoon sesame oil

1 large eggplant, peeled and diced

4 cloves garlic, peeled and minced

½ cup water

¼ cup chopped fresh parsley, divided

¼ teaspoon ground cumin

½ teaspoon salt

2 tablespoons fresh lemon juice

2 tablespoons tahini

1 tablespoon olive oil

¼ teaspoon paprika

1 Press the Sauté button on Instant Pot®. Heat sesame oil. Add eggplant and stir-fry for 4–5 minutes until it softens. Add garlic and cook for an additional minute. Add water. Lock lid.

2 Press the Manual button and adjust time to 4 minutes. When timer beeps, let pressure release naturally until float valve drops and then unlock lid.

3 Strain the cooked eggplant and garlic. Add to a food processor or blender along with ⅛ cup parsley, cumin, salt, lemon juice, and tahini. Pulse to process. Add the olive oil and process until smooth. Transfer to a serving dish and garnish with remaining ⅛ cup chopped parsley and sprinkle with paprika.

Steamed Artichokes with Dipping Sauce

PALEO, GLUTEN-FREE

Not only are artichokes a fun food to eat with other people, but they are an absolute superfood packed with phytonutrients and anti-inflammatory properties helping protect against cancer, heart disease, and diabetes just to name a few. In addition, they help to detoxify your liver.

- **Hands-On Time: 10 minutes**
- **Cook Time: 5 minutes**

Serves 6

6 medium artichokes
1 cup water
3 cloves garlic, quartered
Juice of 1 lemon
1 teaspoon sea salt

INSTANT POT® OPTIONS

Lemon-Herb Butter Dipping Sauce is the perfect dipping sauce to accompany the light nature of the steamed artichoke. To make this recipe, in a small bowl combine 4 tablespoons melted butter or ghee, 2 minced garlic cloves, ½ teaspoon herbes de Provence (or Italian seasoning), 1 tablespoon fresh lemon juice, and a pinch of sea salt and ground pepper.

1 Clean artichokes by clipping off the top third of the leaves and removing the tougher exterior leaves. Trim the bottoms so that they have a flat surface to prop up in the Instant Pot®.

2 Add water, garlic, and lemon juice to Instant Pot®. Set trivet in Instant Pot®. Place artichokes upright in a steamer basket and lower onto the trivet. Sprinkle artichokes with the salt. Lock lid.

3 Press the Manual button and adjust time to 5 minutes. When the timer beeps, quick-release the pressure until the float valve drops and then unlock lid.

4 Lift the artichokes very carefully out of the Instant Pot® (they will be so tender that they may fall apart), transfer to a plate, and serve.

Steamed Vegetable Spring Rolls

These Steamed Vegetable Spring Rolls are a group favorite every time. Pair them with a little chili-lime dipping sauce or even add some diced shrimp or ground chicken to the filling. There are so many possibilities—both savory and sweet—with these magical little spring roll wrappers. And if you're not sure how to wrap these spring rolls, just check out the wrapper packet. It will give you all the information you need to make these rolls amazing.

- **Hands-On Time: 15 minutes**
- **Cook Time: 10 minutes**

Serves 6

1 cup shredded cole slaw mix
  (cabbage and carrots)
2 green onions, thinly sliced
1 cup sliced canned bamboo
  shoots
¼ cup chopped fresh cilantro
2 cloves garlic, peeled and
  minced
¼ cup sliced shiitake
  mushrooms
1 teaspoon honey
1 teaspoon soy sauce
1 teaspoon rice wine vinegar
½ teaspoon fish sauce
½ teaspoon sriracha
¼ teaspoon white pepper
12 (9") spring roll wrappers
2 cups water, divided

1 Combine the cole slaw mix, green onions, bamboo shoots, cilantro, garlic, mushrooms, honey, soy sauce, rice wine vinegar, fish sauce, sriracha, and white pepper in a medium bowl.

2 Press the Sauté button on the Instant Pot® and stir-fry mixture for 3–5 minutes until cabbage is limp. Remove mixture from Instant Pot® and set aside.

3 Working one at a time, quickly dip the spring roll wrappers in ½ cup water and place them on a flat surface.

4 Top each wrapper with an equal amount of the cabbage mixture, making a row down the center. Roll up the wrappers, tuck in the ends, and place side by side in a steamer basket.

5 Add 1½ cups water to Instant Pot®. Add trivet. Lower the steamer basket onto the trivet. Lock lid.

6 Press the Manual button and adjust time to 2 minutes. When timer beeps, let pressure release naturally for 5 minutes. Quick-release any additional pressure until float valve drops and then unlock lid.

7 Remove steamer basket. Serve warm.

Savoy Cabbage Rolls

These little cabbage rolls are a little labor intensive and require some patience. However, if you are up for the challenge, the end result is amazing. Give yourself a pass on the first two rolls but once you get into the swing of things, you'll love the end result!

- **Hands-On Time: 20 minutes**
- **Cook Time: 20 minutes**

Makes 20 rolls

1 medium head savoy
   cabbage
3 cups water, divided
½ pound ground beef
1 cup long-grain rice
1 small red bell pepper,
   seeded and minced
1 medium onion, peeled and
   diced
1 cup beef broth
1 tablespoon olive oil
2 tablespoons minced fresh
   mint
1 teaspoon dried tarragon
1 teaspoon salt
½ teaspoon ground black
   pepper
2 tablespoons lemon juice

1 Wash the cabbage. Remove the large outer leaves and set aside. Remove remaining cabbage leaves and place them in the Instant Pot®. Pour in 1 cup water. Lock lid.

2 Press the Steam button and adjust time to 1 minute. Press the Pressure button to change the pressure to Low. When the timer beeps, quick-release the pressure until float valve drops and then unlock lid. Drain the cabbage leaves in a colander and then move them to a cotton towel.

3 In a medium mixing bowl, add the ground beef, rice, bell pepper, onion, broth, olive oil, mint, tarragon, salt, and pepper. Stir to combine.

4 Place the reserved (uncooked) cabbage leaves on the bottom of the Instant Pot®.

5 Remove the stem running down the center of each steamed cabbage leaf and tear each leaf in half lengthwise. Place 1 tablespoon of the ground beef mixture in the center of each cabbage piece. Loosely fold the sides of the leaf over the filling and then fold the top and bottom of the leaf over the folded sides. As you complete them, place each stuffed cabbage leaf in the Instant Pot®.

6 Pour 2 cups water and the lemon juice over the stuffed cabbage rolls. Lock lid.

7 Press the Manual button and adjust time to 15 minutes. When timer beeps, let pressure release naturally for 10 minutes. Quick-release any additional pressure until float valve drops and then unlock lid.

8 Carefully move the stuffed cabbage rolls to a serving platter. Serve warm.

Georgia Boiled Peanuts

Boiled peanuts can be found every few miles on the backroads in Georgia, next to the watermelon, tomato, and peach stands. If you've never tried this Southern delicacy, pronounced "bowled peanuts," that traditionally takes hours to cook at low heat, just sit back and within 1 hour you'll be serving this Southern delicacy in your own kitchen.

- **Hands-On Time: 5 minutes**
- **Cook Time: 55 minutes**

Serves 8

1 pound raw, unsalted peanuts in the shell
6 cups water
¼ cup salt

1 Rinse and drain the peanuts. Place in Instant Pot®. Add water and salt. Lock lid.

2 Press the Manual button and adjust time to 55 minutes. When the timer beeps, let pressure release naturally for 10 minutes. Quick-release any additional pressure until the float valve drops and then unlock lid.

3 Strain liquid and transfer peanuts to a serving dish with an additional bowl for the shells.

Brown Bag It!

Serve your guests their portion of boiled peanuts in a brown paper lunch bag. It's how you receive them roadside, so why not add some kitschy flair to your own party?

Carne Asada Nachos

PALEO, GLUTEN-FREE

These out-of-this-world Carne Asada Nachos will make everyone think you've been cooking forever . . . when really you've been in the kitchen for under 30 minutes while your Instant Pot® did all of the work! Serve with forks or garnish with chips and pickled jalapeño peppers. Either way, everyone will be happy when they see you show up with this dish at your next get-together. Marinate beef the night before and you'll be good to go.

- **Hands-On Time: 10 minutes**
- **Cook Time: 40 minutes**

Serves 8

2 tablespoons lime juice
2 tablespoons orange juice
1 tablespoon apple cider vinegar
2 tablespoons honey
1 teaspoon ground cumin
2 small jalapeños, seeded and diced
3 cloves garlic, minced
½ cup chopped fresh cilantro
3 tablespoons avocado oil, divided
2 pounds flank steak
1½ cups beef broth

1 In a small bowl, combine lime juice, orange juice, apple cider vinegar, honey, cumin, jalapeños, garlic, cilantro, and 2 tablespoons avocado oil. Spread mixture on all sides of the beef. Refrigerate covered for at least 1 hour or overnight if time allows.

2 Press the Sauté button on Instant Pot®. Heat 1 tablespoon oil. Sear meat 4–5 minutes on each side. Add beef broth. Lock lid.

3 Press the Meat button and cook for the default time of 35 minutes. When the timer beeps, let the pressure release naturally for 5 minutes. Quick-release any additional pressure until the float valve drops and then unlock lid.

4 Remove the meat to a serving platter. Thinly slice and serve.

Pickled Jalapeño Peppers

If you want to use jalapeño peppers as a delicious garnish, consider pickling them! It's quick, easy, and perfect to serve with this recipe. In a small saucepan, combine 6 sliced jalapeños, ¾ cup apple cider vinegar, ½ cup white balsamic vinegar, ¼ cup raw honey, ¼ teaspoon celery seed, ¼ teaspoon garlic powder, and ¼ teaspoon sea salt. Bring to a boil. Reduce heat and let simmer for 5 minutes. Remove from heat until cooled. Refrigerate lidded for 48 hours before serving.

Insalata Caprese Mini Meatballs

This recipe offers a fun twist on not only the traditional party meatball but on the classic insalata caprese. The caprese salad is named for the beautiful isle of Capri and is now loved around the world. The mozzarella used in both the salad and in this dish is now widely made with cow's milk, but if you want to be authentic, find some made from buffalo milk. Now that's Italian!

- **Hands-On Time: 20 minutes**
- **Cook Time: 30 minutes**

Makes 20 meatballs

½ pound ground beef

½ pound ground pork

2 large eggs

1 tablespoon Italian seasoning

1 teaspoon garlic powder

1 teaspoon celery seed

½ teaspoon onion powder

½ teaspoon smoked paprika

½ cup old-fashioned oats

20 mini mozzarella balls (also called *ciliegine*)

3 tablespoons avocado oil, divided

1 (14.5-ounce) can diced tomatoes, drained

2 cups water

20 fresh basil leaves

5 pearl tomatoes, sliced into 20 slices

1 tablespoon olive oil

1 tablespoon balsamic vinegar

1 In a medium bowl, combine beef, pork, eggs, Italian seasoning, garlic powder, celery seed, onion powder, smoked paprika, and oats. Form into 20 meatballs. Press 1 mozzarella ball into the middle of each of the meatballs.

2 Press the Sauté button on the Instant Pot®. Heat 2 tablespoons avocado oil. Place 10 meatballs around the edge of the Instant Pot®. Sear all sides of the meatballs for 3–4 minutes. Remove meatballs from Instant Pot® and set aside. Add the remaining 1 tablespoon avocado oil and sear remaining meatballs for 3–4 minutes. Remove meatballs from Instant Pot® and set aside.

3 Discard extra juice and oil. Add seared meatballs to a 7-cup glass dish. Add drained diced tomatoes.

4 Add 2 cups water to the Instant Pot®. Add trivet. Place the glass dish on top of the trivet. Lock lid.

5 Press the Manual button and adjust time to 20 minutes. When the timer beeps, let pressure release naturally for 10 minutes. Quick-release any additional pressure until float valve drops and then unlock lid.

6 Skewer a meatball, a basil leaf, and a tomato slice on a toothpick. Repeat 20 times. Drizzle skewered meatballs with olive oil and balsamic vinegar. Serve immediately.

Crab and Artichoke Dip

This party dip will have all of your loved ones and guests fighting for more. For a browned top, place the dip under the broiler for 1–3 minutes until it browns to your desired doneness. Serve with tortilla chips, water crackers, or crostini. You can even go old-school and transfer the dip to a hollowed-out round bread loaf.

- **Hands-On Time: 10 minutes**
- **Cook Time: 10 minutes**

Serves 8

16 ounces cream cheese, room temperature

⅛ cup sour cream, room temperature

½ cup minced onion

½ cup seeded and finely diced red bell pepper

½ teaspoon Worcestershire sauce

2 teaspoons prepared horseradish

1 teaspoon Old Bay Seasoning

1 teaspoon sriracha

1 cup diced canned artichoke hearts

¾ pounds lump crabmeat

2 teaspoons lemon zest

¼ teaspoon ground black pepper

¼ cup freshly grated Parmesan cheese, divided

2 cups water

1 Using the tines of two forks, cream together cream cheese and sour cream in a medium bowl until smooth. Add remaining ingredients except ⅛ cup Parmesan cheese and 2 cups water and combine. Spoon into a 7-cup glass dish. Sprinkle top with remaining cheese.

2 Insert trivet into Instant Pot® and pour in 2 cups water. Place glass dish on trivet. Lock lid.

3 Press the Manual button and adjust time to 10 minutes. When timer beeps, quick-release the pressure until float valve drops and then unlock lid. Remove dish and serve warm.

Lentil Pâté

Enjoy this simple and tasty vegetarian version of a French classic. Serve with an assorted tray of cut fresh vegetables or a sliced baguette. A little truffle oil drizzled on top before serving lends a nice, earthy flavor to this dish. Just remember that with truffle oil a little goes a long way, so don't overdo it.

- **Hands-On Time: 5 minutes**
- **Cook Time: 20 minutes**

Serves 10

2 tablespoons olive oil

1 small onion, peeled and diced

1 celery stalk, diced

3 cloves garlic, minced

2 cups dried lentils

4 cups water

1 teaspoon red wine vinegar

2 tablespoons tomato paste

1 teaspoon ground coriander

1 teaspoon ground cumin

1 teaspoon sea salt

1 teaspoon ground black pepper

1 Press Sauté button on Instant Pot®. Heat oil and add onions and celery. Stir-fry for 3–5 minutes until the onions are translucent. Add garlic. Cook for an additional minute. Add remaining ingredients. Lock lid.

2 Press the Manual button and adjust time to 15 minutes. When the timer beeps, let the pressure release naturally for 10 minutes.

3 Quick-release any additional pressure until float valve drops and then unlock lid. Transfer ingredients to a blender or food processor and process until smooth. Spoon into a serving bowl and serve.

Salsa Verde

PALEO, GLUTEN-FREE

Made primarily from tomatillos, Salsa Verde, or "green sauce," is terrific served with chicken enchiladas or even fish tacos. It is also a quick go-to dip served with tortilla chips.

- **Hands-On Time: 5 minutes**
- **Cook Time: 2 minutes**

Serves 8

1 pound tomatillos, outer husks removed

2 small jalapeños, seeded and chopped

1 small onion, peeled and diced

½ cup chopped fresh cilantro

1 teaspoon ground coriander

2 teaspoons sea salt

1½ cups water

1 Cut the tomatillos in half and place in Instant Pot®. Add enough water to cover the tomatillos. Lock lid.

2 Press the Manual button and adjust time to 2 minutes. When timer beeps, let pressure release naturally until float valve drops and then unlock lid.

3 Drain Instant Pot®. Add tomatillos, jalapeños, onion, cilantro, coriander, sea salt, and 1½ cups water to a food processor or blender. Pulse until well combined, about 1–2 minutes.

4 Transfer to a serving dish and chill covered before serving.

Soy Sauce Eggs

With this recipe, you can ditch the traditional deviled eggs and go straight for these modern Asian treats. You can use soy sauce in this recipe, but tamari is thicker and less salty, yielding a less harsh end product. These eggs are also great served with Asian salads or traditional noodle bowls.

- **Hands-On Time: 15 minutes**
- **Cook Time: 7 minutes**

Serves 6

1 cup water
6 large eggs
½ cup tamari
2 tablespoons honey
2 tablespoons rice wine
    vinegar

1   Pour water into Instant Pot®. Lower steamer into pot. Add eggs. Lock lid.

2   Press the Manual button and adjust time to 7 minutes. When timer beeps, quick-release pressure until float valve drops and then unlock lid. Transfer eggs to an ice bath to stop cooking (this also makes them easier to peel).

3   In a medium bowl, whisk together tamari, honey, and rice wine vinegar. Set aside.

4   Peel eggs and marinate in mixture in the refrigerator overnight in a lidded bowl. Cut eggs in half lengthwise and serve.

Mini Potato Skins

These potato skins are so tender when they are first cooked in your Instant Pot® and then finished off in the oven. The smaller red potatoes used here are perfect for bite-sized appetizers for your partygoers to enjoy. Because of the petite size, these skins are an easy bite and seem a little less guilty than a larger potato skin, which will make your guests more likely to indulge!

- **Hands-On Time: 15 minutes**
- **Cook Time: 20 minutes**

Serves 10

2 pounds (about 10) red potatoes, scrubbed

4 tablespoons olive oil

2 sprigs rosemary

1 cup chicken broth

2 tablespoons melted butter

2 cups shredded Cheddar cheese

10 slices bacon, cooked and crumbled

1 cup sour cream

2 green onions, chopped

1 Preheat oven to 350°F.

2 Use a fork to pierce each potato 3 or 4 times. Press the Sauté button on Instant Pot®. Heat oil and add potatoes and rosemary. Coat all sides of potatoes with oil and sauté for about 4–5 minutes until browned. Add broth. Lock lid.

3 Press Manual button and adjust time to 7 minutes. When timer beeps, quick-release pressure until float valve drops and then unlock lid.

4 Let potatoes cool until you can handle them, then discard liquid and rosemary.

5 Cut potatoes in half lengthwise. Scoop out approximately half of the potato creating a boat. Place boats on a baking sheet lined with parchment paper. Thinly brush potatoes with melted butter. Bake for 5 minutes.

6 Distribute cheese among potato halves. Top with cooked, crumbled bacon. Bake skins for an additional 5 minutes until cheese is melted.

7 Remove from oven, top each skin with equal amounts sour cream and green onions, and serve immediately.

6

Side Dishes

On busy nights, sometimes side dishes take the back seat to our busy schedule. And, unfortunately, that usually means the vegetables are kicked to the side. With the Instant Pot®, you can have flavorfully seasoned vegetables in minutes while the main dish is being prepared. Also, pressure cooking vegetables in your Instant Pot® retains more nutrients than boiling them on the stovetop or roasting in the oven does. In addition to these beautifully steamed vegetables, quick pasta dishes like Buttered Egg Noodles can be made with fresh ingredients in the same time that those processed boxed versions can be prepared.

Gingered Sweet Potatoes

This comforting side dish is begging to be put on your holiday table. Depending on the dairy limitations of you or your guests, feel free to use your milk of choice—regular, soy, or almond. Canned coconut milk really gives a fun twist on the taste of these sweet potatoes, so get creative.

- **Hands-On Time: 10 minutes**
- **Cook Time: 10 minutes**

Serves 6

2½ pounds sweet potatoes, peeled and diced large

2 cups water

1 tablespoon minced fresh ginger

½ teaspoon sea salt

1 tablespoon pure maple syrup

1 tablespoon butter

¼ cup milk

1 Add potatoes and water to Instant Pot®. Lock lid.

2 Press the Manual button and adjust time to 10 minutes. When the timer beeps, let the pressure release naturally until the float valve drops and then unlock lid.

3 Drain water from the Instant Pot®. Add remaining ingredients to the potatoes. Using an immersion blender directly in the Instant Pot®, cream the potatoes until desired consistency. Serve warm.

How to Peel Fresh Ginger

Fresh ginger can seem difficult to navigate with its uneven surface and all of the branches. To keep your fingers safe, simply take the edge of a spoon and scrape the peel off of a fresh gingerroot before you grate or mince it.

Maple Dill Carrots

PALEO, GLUTEN-FREE

If you have some leftover turkey or chicken in your refrigerator and need a quick and healthy side dish, this recipe has you covered. It is also worthy to sit beside those other glorious side dishes at your holiday feast—especially if you garnish it with a bit of extra dill. A little sweet and a little savory, these carrots are a delight.

- **Hands-On Time: 10 minutes**
- **Cook Time: 5 minutes**

Serves 6

1 pound carrots, peeled and
    diced large
1 tablespoon minced fresh
    dill
1 tablespoon pure maple
    syrup
1 tablespoon ghee
½ teaspoon sea salt
1 cup water

1 Add all ingredients to Instant Pot®. Lock lid.

2 Press the Manual button and adjust time to 5 minutes. When the timer beeps, let the pressure release naturally until the float valve drops and then unlock lid.

3 Transfer to a serving dish and serve warm.

Swiss Chard and Vegetables in Parmesan Sauce

Aside from being quick and easy to make, this rich side dish is incredibly versatile. Serve it with Italian-seasoned grilled chicken breast or veal cutlets or pair it with something as simple as leftover roast turkey or chicken.

- **Hands-On Time: 15 minutes**
- **Cook Time: 15 minutes**

Serves 8

2 tablespoons olive oil

1 small onion, peeled and sliced

3 stalks celery, diced

2 medium carrots, peeled and sliced

4 cloves garlic, minced

1 head cauliflower, chopped into florets

1 pound Brussels sprouts, cleaned and halved

1 medium zucchini, diced large

1 pound Swiss chard, cleaned, deveined, and chopped

1 cup water

½ cup heavy cream

1 tablespoon flour

4 tablespoons butter

½ cup grated Parmesan cheese

⅛ teaspoon red pepper flakes

1 Press the Sauté button on the Instant Pot® and heat oil. Add onion, celery, and carrots. Stir-fry 3–5 minutes until onions are translucent. Add garlic. Cook for an additional minute.

2 Add a layer of cauliflower, a layer of Brussels sprouts, a layer of zucchini, and a layer of Swiss chard. Gently pour in 1 cup water. Lock lid.

3 Press the Manual button and adjust time to 3 minutes.

4 While vegetables are cooking, in a small bowl whisk together heavy cream and flour to create a slurry. Set aside.

5 When Instant Pot® timer beeps, quick-release the pressure until the float valve drops and then unlock lid. Drain the vegetables, reserving liquid. Add 2 tablespoons reserved cooking liquid, butter, Parmesan cheese, red pepper flakes, and heavy cream slurry to vegetables in the Instant Pot®. Stir and let warm unlidded for 5 minutes until sauce thickens. Add more reserved cooking liquid if needed. Transfer vegetables and sauce to a serving bowl and serve warm.

Garlicky Mashed Root Vegetables

PALEO, GLUTEN-FREE

There are many underrated root vegetables out there, and this recipe is your introduction to the many textures and flavors of these less popular varieties. Play around with the amounts of the different vegetables in your mash, but definitely join the game, because each one brings a different nutritional résumé to the table.

- **Hands-On Time: 15 minutes**
- **Cook Time: 5 minutes**

Serves 4

- **2 medium turnips, peeled and diced**
- **2 medium parsnips, peeled and diced**
- **1 large Yukon gold potato, peeled and diced**
- **3 cloves garlic, peeled and halved**
- **1 medium shallot, peeled and quartered**
- **½ cup chicken broth**
- **1 cup water**
- **¼ cup unsweetened almond milk**
- **2 tablespoons ghee**
- **½ teaspoon sea salt**
- **½ teaspoon ground black pepper**

1 Add the turnips, parsnips, potato, garlic, shallot, broth, and water to Instant Pot®. Lock lid.

2 Press the Manual button and adjust time to 5 minutes. When timer beeps, let pressure release naturally for 10 minutes. Quick-release any additional pressure until the float valve drops and then unlock lid.

3 Transfer vegetables to a medium bowl. Add milk, ghee, salt, and pepper. Using a hand-held mixer or immersion blender, purée mixture until smooth. Add additional broth 1 tablespoon at a time from the Instant Pot® if mixture is too thick. Serve warm.

Homemade Almond Milk

To make almond milk at home, all you have to do is follow these simple instructions. To start, soak almonds in water for at least 24 hours, then rinse and drain. In a stand blender or food processor, pulse 1¾ cups water and 1 cup unsalted, raw almonds. Strain the liquid through a fine sieve or cheesecloth, then either refrigerate up to 2–3 days or use immediately.

Citrus-Bacon Brussels Sprouts

PALEO, GLUTEN-FREE

Although a great source of vitamins C and K, Brussels sprouts are usually a love 'em or leave 'em vegetable. But this recipe will make giving this vegetable one more chance worth your while. This dish pairs nicely with a roasted potato and Cornish hen meal—and a crisp glass of chardonnay, of course.

- **Hands-On Time: 5 minutes**
- **Cook Time: 8 minutes**

Serves 4

1 tablespoon avocado oil
2 slices bacon, diced
½ cup freshly squeezed
    orange juice
½ cup water
1 pound Brussels sprouts,
    trimmed and halved
2 teaspoons orange zest

1   Press the Sauté button on Instant Pot® and heat avocado oil. Add bacon. Stir-fry 3–5 minutes or until bacon is almost crisp and the fat is rendered. Add the orange juice and water and deglaze the Instant Pot® by scraping the bits from the sides and bottom of the Instant Pot®.

2   Add Brussels sprouts. Lock lid.

3   Press the "Manual" button and adjust time to 3 minutes. When timer beeps, quick-release pressure until the float valve drops and then unlock lid.

4   Using a slotted spoon, transfer Brussels sprouts to a serving dish. Garnish with orange zest and serve warm.

Brussels Sprouts?

Have you ever wondered why some people just seem to shovel those beautiful little cabbages into their mouth with glee and you turn your nose up? Well, it just may be in your DNA. Not everyone's taste receptors receive Brussels sprouts in the same way, similar to how some people love cilantro while others can't stomach it.

Garlic and Chive Home Fries

PALEO, GLUTEN-FREE

These amazing Garlic and Chive Home Fries are great in their very own bowl or alongside a simple and tasty beef dish. You can peel the potatoes if you'd prefer, but leaving the skin on lends a rustic feel to this dish and makes it easier to prepare. You can serve this either way, but no matter what you choose this delicious recipe transforms the simple potato into a side dish that everyone will enjoy.

- **Hands-On Time: 5 minutes**
- **Cook Time: 10 minutes**

Serves 4

½ cup chicken broth
4 cups cubed sweet potatoes
2 tablespoons ghee
3 cloves garlic, minced
1 teaspoon paprika
1 teaspoon sea salt
½ teaspoon ground black pepper
1 tablespoon chopped fresh chives

1 Place a metal steamer into your Instant Pot®. Pour in chicken broth. Add potatoes to the steamer. Lock lid.

2 Press the Manual button and adjust time to 5 minutes. When timer beeps, let pressure release naturally for 10 minutes. Quick-release any additional pressure until float valve drops and then unlock lid.

3 Remove potatoes and steamer from the pot. Set potatoes aside. Discard broth.

4 Press the Sauté button on the Instant Pot®. Heat ghee. Add the potatoes and stir-fry for 3–5 minutes until browned. Add garlic and heat an additional minute. Transfer potatoes to a bowl and toss with paprika, salt, and pepper. Garnish with chives and serve warm.

Mustard Potato Salad

Homemade potato salad can be a pain when you have to boil both potatoes and eggs. You have different timers. You dirty up several dishes. Fortunately, the Instant Pot® allows you to cook your potatoes and eggs in the same pot in just minutes. When it's this easy to make something so perfect, you'll quickly find that this recipe becomes your go-to picnic side dish.

- **Hands-On Time: 10 minutes**
- **Cook Time: 5 minutes**

Serves 8

1 pound (about 5 medium) red potatoes, cut in ½" cubes
½ cup broth
3 large eggs
8–10 ice cubes
1 cup water
1 cup mayonnaise
1 teaspoon apple cider vinegar
1 tablespoon yellow mustard
½ cup chopped celery
½ cup peeled and chopped onion
1 tablespoon dill relish
¼ teaspoon fine sea salt
¼ teaspoon celery salt
½ teaspoon smoked paprika
½ teaspoon ground black pepper

1 Place potatoes in the Instant Pot®. Add broth. Nestle the eggs in the potatoes. Lock lid.

2 Press the Manual button and adjust time to 5 minutes. When timer beeps, quick-release pressure until float valve drops and then unlock lid.

3 Transfer eggs to an iced water bath by placing 8–10 ice cubes in a medium bowl filled with about 1 cup of water leaving enough room to add eggs. Drain potatoes and set aside.

4 In a medium bowl, combine mayonnaise, vinegar, yellow mustard, celery, onion, dill relish, salt, celery salt, smoked paprika, and black pepper. Peel eggs and dice. Add to mayonnaise mixture. Add potatoes. Carefully toss.

5 Refrigerate lidded until ready to serve chilled.

Bacon Red Cabbage with Goat Cheese

GLUTEN-FREE

The salt from the bacon and the creaminess of the goat cheese help counter any possible bitterness some may generally detect in red cabbage. The apple cider vinegar helps temper this as well. The vinegar also works with collard and turnip greens.

- **Hands-On Time: 10 minutes**
- **Cook Time: 20 minutes**

Serves 4

1 tablespoon olive oil

1 small onion, peeled and diced

3 slices bacon, diced

1 small apple, peeled, cored, and diced

5 cups chopped red cabbage

1 cup chicken broth

½ cup apple cider vinegar

½ teaspoon sea salt

¼ cup crumbled goat cheese

1 Press the Sauté button on Instant Pot®. Heat olive oil. Add the onion and sauté for 3–5 minutes until translucent. Add bacon and stir-fry an additional 3 minutes until the bacon starts to crisp. Toss in apple and cabbage. Add broth and vinegar. Lock lid.

2 Press the Manual button and adjust time to 10 minutes. When the timer beeps, quick-release pressure until the float valve drops and then unlock lid.

3 Using a slotted spoon, transfer ingredients to a serving plate. Let cool for 10 minutes. Toss in salt and garnish with goat cheese. Serve warm.

Creamy Creamed Corn

Take that fresh summer corn to the next level with this traditional recipe. This creamy side dish is perfect served with whatever you have going on the grill, and it's sure to put a smile on the faces of everyone who tries it.

- **Hands-On Time: 15 minutes**
- **Cook Time: 7 minutes**

Serves 6

6 large ears of corn or 8 medium, husked
½ cup water
½ teaspoon sea salt
½ teaspoon ground black pepper
4 ounces cream cheese, cubed and room temperature
4 tablespoons ghee, cubed and room temperature
1 teaspoon sugar
1 cup heavy cream
1 tablespoon flour

1 Cut off the corn kernels from the cob, really scraping the cobs to release that milky substance. Place the kernels, water, salt, pepper, cream cheese, ghee, and sugar in the Instant Pot®. Lock lid.

2 Press the Manual button and adjust time to 2 minutes.

3 In a small bowl, whisk together the heavy cream and flour to create a slurry.

4 When timer beeps, quick-release the pressure until the float valve drops and then unlock lid. Add the slurry to the corn in the Instant Pot® and stir. Press the Keep Warm button and warm unlidded for 5 minutes to thicken.

5 Transfer to a medium bowl and serve warm.

Burgundy Mushrooms

PALEO, GLUTEN-FREE

These Burgundy Mushrooms are a side dish you'll find yourself making again and again. Don't skip the bacon in this recipe as the meatiness and saltiness adds a deep flavor to this insanely, richly flavored earthy side dish. Serve alongside a grilled steak with some Garlicky Mashed Root Vegetables (see recipe in this chapter) and you'll have a meal to be proud of.

- **Hands-On Time: 5 minutes**
- **Cook Time: 30 minutes**

Serves 8

½ cup ghee

3 cloves garlic, halved

16 ounces whole white mushrooms

16 ounces whole baby bella mushrooms

1½ cups dry red wine

1 teaspoon Worcestershire sauce

1 teaspoon dried thyme

1 tablespoon Dijon mustard

1 teaspoon ground celery seed

½ teaspoon ground black pepper

3 cups beef broth

2 slices bacon

1 Press the Sauté button on the Instant Pot®. Add ghee and melt. Add garlic and mushrooms and toss to coat with butter. Stir-fry for 3 minutes until mushrooms start to get tender. Add red wine, press Sauté button, press Adjust button to change temperature to Less, and simmer for 5 minutes.

2 Place remaining ingredients into Instant Pot®. Lock lid.

3 Press the Manual button and adjust time to 20 minutes. When timer beeps, let pressure release naturally until float valve drops and then unlock lid. Discard bacon and garlic.

4 Using a slotted spoon, remove mushrooms and transfer to a serving bowl. Serve warm.

Cranberry-Orange Sauce

Nothing says the holidays like cranberry sauce. But don't even think about buying that jiggly canned stuff when this fresh sauce can be yours in minutes. In this upscale sauce, the citrus from the orange lends another level of flavor and sweetness that pairs nicely with the tartness of the berries. You'll never eat cranberry sauce from a can again—guaranteed.

- **Hands-On Time: 5 minutes**
- **Cook Time: 1 minute**

Serves 8

4 cups fresh cranberries
½ cup canned crushed
    pineapple
Juice from 1 orange
2 teaspoons orange zest
½ cup pure maple syrup
¼ teaspoon cinnamon
Pinch of salt
2 tablespoons sugar

1 Add all ingredients to Instant Pot®. Lock lid.

2 Press the Manual button and adjust time to 1 minute. When timer beeps, let pressure release naturally until float valve drops and then unlock lid.

3 Stir ingredients in the Instant Pot® and smash any unpopped cranberries with the back of a wooden spoon. Transfer sauce to a serving dish and serve warm.

Lucky Collard Greens

PALEO, GLUTEN-FREE

Collard greens are a sure way to help bring you economic fortune for the New Year—or at least that's how the story goes. Resembling folded money, greens are consumed on January 1 by millions of people in a variety of countries. Enjoy a scoop of this next to a serving of Hoppin' John (see recipe in Chapter 4).

- **Hands-On Time: 10 minutes**
- **Cook Time: 10 minutes**

Serves 6

2 pounds collard greens, washed, spines removed, and chopped
1 small onion, peeled and diced
1 cup chicken broth
¼ cup apple cider vinegar
1 teaspoon sriracha
1 slice bacon
½ teaspoon sea salt
¼ teaspoon ground black pepper

1 Place all ingredients in Instant Pot®. Lock lid.

2 Press the Manual button and adjust time to 10 minutes. When the timer beeps, let pressure release naturally until float valve drops and then unlock lid. Discard bacon.

3 Using a slotted spoon, transfer collard greens to a dish and serve warm.

Can I Use Other Greens in This Dish?

Greens are greens when it comes to the economic luck that will follow you through the year. Chard, turnip greens, mustard greens, and kale can all be substituted in this recipe or use a blend of your favorites. Just be sure to give these leaves a good cleaning and cut out those tough spines.

Steamed Broccoli

PALEO, GLUTEN-FREE

Serve this Steamed Broccoli alongside any meal and enjoy the health benefits of this cabbage family member. Low in calories and high in phytonutrients, broccoli is a superfood that will help protect your body against a variety of cancers.

- **Hands-On Time: 5 minutes**
- **Cook Time: 0 minutes (it will cook while the pressure builds)**

Serves 4

1 cup water
1 medium head broccoli, chopped
1 teaspoon lemon juice
½ teaspoon sea salt
2 teaspoons ghee

1 Pour water into Instant Pot®. Insert a steamer basket and arrange broccoli on the basket in an even layer. Lock lid.

2 Press the Steam button and adjust time to 0 minutes. The broccoli will steam in the time it takes the pressure to build. When timer beeps, quick-release pressure until float valve drops and then unlock lid.

3 Use retriever tongs to remove steamer basket. Transfer broccoli to a serving dish and toss with lemon juice, salt, and ghee. Serve warm.

Diced Turnips and Greens

PALEO, GLUTEN-FREE

Don't forget about the incredibly nutritious turnip greens tops when cooking turnips. The saltiness of the ham hock adds a happy dimension to this dish, and the vinegar helps combat the natural bitterness of the greens. The touch of honey rounds out that saltiness, acidity, and bitterness, making this a completely balanced side dish.

- **Hands-On Time: 10 minutes**
- **Cook Time: 10 minutes**

Serves 4

4 small turnips with turnip
greens
1 small onion, peeled and
diced
1 cup chicken broth
¼ cup apple cider vinegar
1 tablespoon honey
1 teaspoon sriracha
1 ham hock
¼ teaspoon ground black
pepper

1   Wash turnips. Peel and dice. Wash turnip greens. Cut out stems and spines. Dice leaves.

2   Place all ingredients in Instant Pot®. Lock lid.

3   Press the Manual button and adjust time to 10 minutes. When timer beeps, let the pressure release naturally until float valve drops and then unlock lid. Remove ham hock, pull meat off of the bone, and dice. Add meat back to Instant Pot®. Discard bone.

4   Using a slotted spoon, transfer turnip greens, turnips, and ham to a serving dish. Serve warm.

Chilled Pearl Couscous Salad

Also known as Israeli couscous, this larger-grain pearl couscous is the perfect one to use for this refreshing side salad. The larger grains lend more substance than its smaller counterpart. Combined with the acidity and sweetness from the orange juice and the freshness from the cucumber, pepper, and tomatoes, this dish will keep you coming back for more.

- **Hands-On Time: 15 minutes**
- **Cook Time: 10 minutes**

Serves 6

3 tablespoons olive oil, divided

1 cup pearl couscous

1 cup water

1 cup fresh orange juice

1 small cucumber, seeded and diced

1 small yellow bell pepper, seeded and diced

2 small Roma tomatoes, seeded and diced

¼ cup slivered almonds

¼ cup chopped fresh mint leaves

2 tablespoons lemon juice

1 teaspoon lemon zest

¼ cup feta cheese

¼ teaspoon fine sea salt

1 teaspoon smoked paprika

1 teaspoon garlic powder

1 Press the Sauté button on the Instant Pot®. Heat 1 tablespoon olive oil, add couscous, and stir-fry for 2–4 minutes until couscous is slightly browned. Add water and orange juice. Lock lid.

2 Press the Manual button and adjust time to 5 minutes. When the timer beeps, let pressure release naturally for 5 minutes. Quick-release any additional pressure until float valve drops and then unlock lid. Drain any liquid.

3 Combine remaining ingredients in a medium bowl. Set aside. Once couscous has cooled, toss it into bowl ingredients. Cover and refrigerate overnight until ready to serve chilled.

Chow-Chow Relish

A Southern staple, this Chow-Chow Relish will transform pretty much all of your existing recipes by adding another dimension of sweet and sour flavors. Add a dollop to your hot dog, fish tacos, alongside a pork chop, or even to tuna salad.

- **Hands-On Time: 15 minutes**
- **Cook Time: 20 minutes**

Serves 8

2 large green bell peppers, seeded and diced small

1 large red bell pepper, seeded and diced small

2 large green tomatoes, diced small

2 cups finely diced cabbage

1 large sweet onion, peeled and diced small

1 tablespoon ground mustard

2 teaspoons red pepper flakes

2 teaspoons celery seed

2 teaspoons ground ginger

1 teaspoon ground turmeric

1 tablespoon sea salt

½ cup granulated sugar

½ cup packed dark brown sugar

1 cup apple cider vinegar

1 cup water

1 Place all ingredients into Instant Pot®. Lock lid.

2 Press the Manual button and adjust time to 20 minutes. When timer beeps, let pressure release naturally until float valve drops and then unlock lid. Stir.

3 Use a slotted spoon to transfer relish to a serving dish. Serve warmed or chilled.

Buttered Egg Noodles

This creamy side dish is always a family favorite. Maybe it takes your memories back to that traditional beef stroganoff and tuna casserole that mom used to make. Serve these glorious noodles simply with chicken or steak and add a side of steamed broccoli for a well-rounded meal.

- **Hands-On Time: 2 minutes**
- **Cook Time: 4 minutes**

Serves 6

1 (12-ounce) bag egg noodles
3 tablespoons butter
¼ cup grated Parmesan cheese
½ teaspoon sea salt
¼ teaspoon ground black pepper
¼ cup chopped fresh parsley

1 Place noodles in an even layer in Instant Pot®. Pour enough water to come about ¼" over pasta. Lock lid.

2 Press the Manual button and adjust time to 4 minutes. When timer beeps, unplug the Instant Pot® and let pressure release naturally for 3 minutes. Quick-release any additional pressure until float valve drops and then unlock lid.

3 Drain any residual water. Toss pasta with butter, Parmesan cheese, salt, pepper, and parsley. Serve immediately.

Chicken Main Dishes

Chicken is probably one of the most consumed proteins in the United States. There are a million recipes and a handful of go-to meals that you can cook for your family. But if you're sick of eating dried-out chicken breast and overcooked thighs, the Instant Pot® is your new best friend. The steam and pressure used to cook items in the pot are guaranteed to leave the chicken dishes in this chapter juicy and delicious! Whether you're craving Beer Can Chicken Dijon or Herbed Chicken in Lemon Sauce, or your family is calling for Chili Lime Chicken or Bourbon Barbecue Chicken, you'll find a new favorite recipe here!

Let your Instant Pot® release its pressure naturally for these recipes for 5–10 minutes, as doing an immediate quick release can let that moisture escape not only from your pot but from your chicken as well. And if you're planning on getting home late, the Instant Pot® allows you to start a meal in the morning and set it to automatically switch to the Keep Warm function for up to 10 hours, which means dinner will be ready and waiting when you walk in the door. So get cooking!

Simple Whole Chicken

PALEO, GLUTEN-FREE

If you are a "prep day" person, put this recipe on your list. Making a whole chicken and then using the carcass to make broth (see recipe in Chapter 3) afterward is a tasty and inexpensive way to stretch your dollar during the week. The chicken can be eaten as is or served in any number of chicken dishes including simple wraps, on top of salads, or even as a great base for other recipes in this chapter.

- **Hands-On Time: 10 minutes**
- **Cook Time: 25 minutes**

Serves 4

1 (5-pound) whole chicken
2 teaspoons sea salt
1 teaspoon ground black pepper
1 medium apple, peeled, quartered, and cored
1 medium onion, peeled and roughly chopped
3 cloves garlic, halved
1 celery stalk, chopped
2 large carrots, peeled and chopped
3 sprigs thyme
2 cups water

1 Pat the chicken dry, inside and out, with paper towels. Sprinkle chicken with salt and pepper, then place the apple in the cavity of the bird.

2 In the bottom of the Instant Pot®, scatter the onion, garlic, celery, carrots, and thyme. Pour in the water. Place the trivet over the vegetables.

3 Place chicken on the trivet. Lock lid.

4 Press the Manual button and adjust time to 25 minutes. When timer beeps, let pressure release naturally until float valve drops and then unlock lid. Check the chicken using a meat thermometer to ensure the internal temperature is at least 165°F.

5 Remove chicken and vegetables. Discard apple. Serve warm.

Chicken at 165°F

The USDA has deemed 165°F to be the magic number that will effectively kill any possible viruses and pathogens that may possibly be present in poultry dishes. The meat thermometer is one of the most inexpensive, yet crucial, kitchen tools. You can feel confident that your meats are cooked to a correct temperature and won't come out dry and overcooked.

Asian Sesame Chicken

PALEO, GLUTEN-FREE

Serve this Asian dish by itself, over rice, or even over some spiraled sweet potatoes. Just peel two sweet potatoes, spiral, and do a quick sauté with about one teaspoon of sesame oil until potatoes are tender.

- **Hands-On Time: 10 minutes**
- **Cook Time: 25 minutes**

Serves 6

¼ cup coconut aminos

¼ cup tomato sauce

½ cup honey

2 teaspoons fish sauce

1 teaspoon hot sauce

¼ teaspoon white pepper

2 pounds boneless chicken thighs, cut into 1" cubes

1 tablespoon sesame oil

1 small onion, peeled and diced

3 cloves garlic, minced

1 tablespoon arrowroot powder

1 tablespoon water

3 green onions, sliced (white and green parts)

1 tablespoon toasted sesame seeds

1 In a medium bowl, whisk together coconut aminos, tomato sauce, honey, fish sauce, hot sauce, and white pepper. Toss chicken to coat. Set aside in the refrigerator.

2 Press the Sauté button on the Instant Pot® and heat sesame oil. Add onion and garlic and sauté for about 3–5 minutes until onions are translucent. Add chicken and all of the sauce into the onion mixture. Toss to coat. Lock lid.

3 Press the Poultry button and cook for the default time of 15 minutes. When timer beeps, let pressure release naturally for 10 minutes. Quick-release any additional pressure until float valve drops and then unlock lid. Check the chicken using a meat thermometer to ensure the internal temperature is at least 165°F. Using a slotted spoon, transfer chicken to a serving platter.

4 In a small bowl, whisk together arrowroot powder and water to create a slurry. Stir this into sauce in the Instant Pot®. Press the Sauté button, press the Adjust button to change the temperature to Less, and simmer unlidded for 5 minutes to thicken the sauce.

5 Pour desired amount of sauce over chicken and garnish with sliced green onions and sesame seeds.

Easy Pesto Chicken and Red Potatoes

There's something to be said for a dish that not only tastes delicious but smells delicious, too. And this recipe gives you the best of both worlds. In addition, this pesto chicken is incredibly quick and easy to make. This is one of those go-to recipes that you'll find yourself impressing your family with at least once a week.

- **Hands-On Time: 5 minutes**
- **Cook Time: 10 minutes**

Serves 8

3 pounds boneless chicken thighs
¾ cup pesto
2 pounds (8 medium) red potatoes, quartered
1 large sweet onion, peeled and chopped
1 cup chicken broth

1 Place chicken in a bowl or plastic bag. Add pesto. Toss or shake chicken to distribute the pesto evenly over the thighs. Set aside in the refrigerator.

2 Layer potatoes and onions in the Instant Pot®. Pour in the chicken broth. Place chicken on top. Lock lid.

3 Press the Manual button and adjust time to 10 minutes. When timer beeps, let pressure release naturally for 10 minutes. Quick-release any additional pressure until float valve drops and then unlock lid. Check the chicken using a meat thermometer to ensure the internal temperature is at least 165°F.

4 Using a slotted spoon, remove chicken and potatoes and transfer to a platter. Discard liquid. Serve warm.

The Ins and Outs of Pesto

If you have an herb garden or just like to make your own items, pesto is so easy to make. Just pulse the following ingredients in a small food processor: 1 cup fresh basil leaves, 1 cup fresh parsley leaves, ½ cup extra-virgin olive oil, ⅓ cup pine nuts, ½ cup freshly grated Parmesan, 3–5 cloves garlic, ½ teaspoon sea salt, and ¼ teaspoon ground black pepper. Now here's where the fun happens. You don't need the cheese. You can sub out the herbs and nuts. Feel free to go crazy!

Herbed Chicken in Lemon Sauce

PALEO, GLUTEN-FREE

There is a reason that herbs, lemon, and chicken have been a trinity for so long. This trio just tastes good. Add the Instant Pot® to this threesome and you'll get the impeccable flavor of this combination with tender, moist chicken to boot.

- **Hands-On Time: 5 minutes**
- **Cook Time: 25 minutes**

Serves 4

2 tablespoons avocado oil

1 pound boneless, skinless chicken breast, cut in 1" cubes

1 teaspoon sea salt

½ cup chicken broth

2 tablespoons fresh lemon juice

2 cloves garlic, minced

2 teaspoons Dijon mustard

1 tablespoon Italian seasoning

1 tablespoon lemon zest

¼ cup chopped fresh parsley

1 Press the Sauté button on the Instant Pot®. Heat the oil and add the chicken pieces. Stir-fry for about 4 minutes or until lightly browned on all sides. Stir in remaining ingredients except for lemon zest and chopped parsley. Lock lid.

2 Press the Poultry button and cook for the default time of 15 minutes. When timer beeps, let the pressure release naturally for 10 minutes. Quick-release any additional pressure until the float valve drops and then unlock lid. Check the chicken using a meat thermometer to ensure the internal temperature is at least 165°F. Transfer chicken to a serving platter.

3 Press the Sauté button, press the Adjust button to change the temperature to Less, and simmer unlidded for 5 minutes to thicken sauce in the Instant Pot®; then pour sauce over chicken.

4 Garnish with lemon zest and chopped parsley. Serve warm.

Chicken Breast Parmesan with Mushrooms

Who doesn't love chicken parmesan? This allergy-conscious dish leaves out all the gluten but retains the flavor of the original recipe. This tomato-based dish is perfect ladled over a bowl of pasta or spiraled zucchini noodles or eaten on its own. No matter what you choose to do, you're guaranteed to be happy with your delicious decision to try this recipe.

- **Hands-On Time: 15 minutes**
- **Cook Time: 20 minutes**

Serves 8

½ cup all-purpose flour
½ teaspoon salt
½ teaspoon ground black pepper
2 pounds boneless, skinless chicken breast, cut in 1" cubes
2 tablespoons olive oil
1 large onion, peeled and diced
1 tablespoon Italian seasoning
2 tablespoons tomato paste
½ cup chicken broth
1 (8-ounce) can tomato sauce
1 teaspoon balsamic vinegar
2 cups sliced white mushrooms
2 teaspoons honey
2 tablespoons chopped fresh parsley
1 cup grated Parmesan cheese

1 Add the flour, salt, and pepper to a large zip-closure bag; seal and shake to mix. Add chicken cubes to the bag, seal, and shake to coat the meat in the flour.

2 Press the Sauté button on the Instant Pot®. Heat the oil and add the chicken and onion. Stir-fry for 3–5 minutes until onions are translucent. Stir in Italian seasoning and tomato paste. Sauté for 2 minutes. Stir in the broth, tomato sauce, vinegar, mushrooms, and honey. Lock lid.

3 Press the Manual button and adjust time to 12 minutes. When timer beeps, let pressure release naturally for 10 minutes. Quick-release any additional pressure until float valve drops and then unlock lid. Check the chicken using a meat thermometer to ensure the internal temperature is at least 165°F.

4 Stir the cooked chicken and sauce in the Instant Pot®. Transfer to a serving dish. Garnish with parsley and grated Parmesan cheese and serve warm.

Chicken Paprikash

Of Hungarian origin, this easy-to-make chicken recipe takes hardly any time or effort at all. Chicken Paprikash simply means paprika chicken. Serve it over buttered egg noodles or spiraled zucchini noodles and top with additional sour cream and some chopped green onions to really make this dish a meal.

- **Hands-On Time: 10 minutes**
- **Cook Time: 25 minutes**

Serves 4

2 tablespoons ghee
1 medium onion, peeled and diced
1 small green bell pepper, seeded and diced
4 cloves garlic, minced
4 skin-on chicken breast halves (about 2 pounds)
1 large tomato, diced
¼ cup tomato sauce
2 tablespoons Hungarian paprika
1 cup chicken broth
1 tablespoon flour
¾ cup sour cream
½ teaspoon sea salt
¼ teaspoon ground black pepper

1 Press the Sauté button on the Instant Pot® and heat ghee. Add onion and green pepper and sauté for 3–5 minutes until onions are translucent. Stir in garlic. Add the chicken breast skin-side down and brown for 3–4 minutes. Sprinkle the diced tomato over the chicken.

2 In a medium bowl, whisk together tomato sauce, paprika, and chicken broth. Pour over chicken. Lock lid.

3 Press the Poultry button and cook for the default time of 15 minutes. When timer beeps, let pressure release naturally for 10 minutes. Quick-release any additional pressure until float valve drops and then unlock lid. Check the chicken using a meat thermometer to ensure the internal temperature is at least 165°F. Transfer chicken to a serving platter.

4 Whisk flour and sour cream into the juices in the Instant Pot®. Press the Sauté button, press the Adjust button to change the temperature to Less, and simmer unlidded for 5 minutes until sauce thickens. Season with salt and pepper. Pour sauce over chicken and serve warm.

Chicken alla Diavola

Chicken alla Diavola translates as "the devil's chicken," and the spice in this dish is where it gets the name. Serve this to the heat seekers in your life for a fireball of a good time.

- **Hands-On Time: 10 minutes**
- **Cook Time: 20 minutes**

Serves 4

1 teaspoon sea salt

2 cloves garlic, minced

2 tablespoons apple cider vinegar

4 tablespoons olive oil, divided

1 teaspoon sriracha

1 teaspoon chili powder

¼ teaspoon cayenne pepper

1 pound boneless, skinless chicken breast, cut in 1" cubes

2 cups water

1 In a medium bowl, whisk together salt, garlic, vinegar, 2 tablespoons oil, sriracha, chili powder, and cayenne pepper. Toss chicken into mixture and coat evenly. Cover and refrigerate for 1 hour.

2 Press the Sauté button on the Instant Pot®. Heat remaining 2 tablespoons oil and add the chicken pieces. Stir-fry for about 4 minutes or until browned on all sides. Remove chicken and set aside.

3 Insert trivet into Instant Pot®. Add water. Transfer chicken to a large square (about 10" × 10") of aluminum foil. Set the foil onto the trivet. Lock lid.

4 Press the Poultry button and cook for the default time of 15 minutes. When timer beeps, let pressure release naturally for 10 minutes. Quick-release any additional pressure until float valve drops and then unlock lid. Check the chicken using a meat thermometer to ensure the internal temperature is at least 165°F. Serve warm.

Chili Lime Chicken

PALEO, GLUTEN-FREE

Your taste buds won't know what to make of this ridiculously easy-to-make chicken dish. Is it hot? Is it sweet? Is it sour? Yes to all three! Serve this with some simply steamed veggies on the side and heat up any leftovers for a great lunch to take to work.

- **Hands-On Time: 5 minutes**
- **Cook Time: 10 minutes**

Serves 8

½ cup fresh lime juice
Zest from 1 lime
¼ cup olive oil
2 small jalapeños, seeded and finely chopped
3 garlic cloves, minced
2 tablespoons honey
2 teaspoons sea salt
2 teaspoons chili powder
¼ cup finely chopped fresh cilantro
3 pounds boneless chicken thighs
1 cup chicken broth

1 In a large bowl, combine all ingredients except for chicken and chicken broth.

2 Pat chicken thighs dry with a paper towel. Toss chicken into marinade. Cover and refrigerate overnight.

3 Place trivet in Instant Pot®. Place steamer basket on trivet. Pour in chicken broth. Arrange thighs on steamer basket and pour extra marinade over the thighs. Lock lid.

4 Press the Manual button and adjust time to 10 minutes. When timer beeps, let pressure release naturally for 10 minutes. Quick-release any additional pressure until float valve drops and then unlock lid. Check the chicken using a meat thermometer to ensure the internal temperature is at least 165°F.

5 Transfer chicken to plates and serve warm.

Chicken Marinara and Zucchini

Do you ever have those days when you just need to throw a meal together on the fly? Whether you use homemade or jarred marinara sauce, this quick meal uses what you already have on hand, turning basic ingredients into an Italian dream in minutes on the hour.

- **Hands-On Time: 5 minutes**
- **Cook Time: 15 minutes**

Serves 4

2 large zucchini, diced large

4 chicken breast halves (about 2 pounds)

3 cups marinara sauce

1 tablespoon Italian seasoning

½ teaspoon sea salt

1 cup shredded mozzarella

1 Scatter zucchini into Instant Pot®. Place chicken on zucchini. Pour marinara sauce over chicken. Sprinkle with Italian seasoning and salt. Lock lid.

2 Press the Poultry button and cook for the default time of 15 minutes. When timer beeps, let pressure release naturally for 10 minutes. Quick-release any additional pressure until float valve drops and then unlock lid. Check chicken using a meat thermometer to ensure the internal temperature is at least 165°F.

3 Sprinkle chicken with mozzarella. Press Keep Warm button, lock lid back in place, and warm for 5 minutes to allow the cheese to melt.

4 Transfer chicken and zucchini to a serving platter.

Buffalo Chicken Wraps

These Buffalo Chicken Wraps are a great twist on a bar menu classic. Make them for dinner and then pack one for lunch the next day. If you're serving a crowd, just double or triple the recipe and cut the wraps into thirds to present wrap bites to your guests as a bite-sized appetizer.

- **Hands-On Time: 10 minutes**
- **Cook Time: 20 minutes**

8 servings

2 cups buffalo wing sauce

2 tablespoons melted butter

2 pounds chicken breasts, halved

8 (8") flour tortillas

1 cup finely diced celery, divided

8 tablespoons blue cheese dressing

1 In a large bowl, whisk together wing sauce and butter. Add chicken breasts and toss to coat. Place chicken and all of the sauce in the Instant Pot®. Lock lid.

2 Press the Manual button and adjust time to 20 minutes. When the timer beeps, let pressure release naturally for 10 minutes. Quick-release any additional pressure until float valve drops and then unlock lid. Check the chicken using a meat thermometer to ensure the internal temperature is at least 165°F.

3 With the chicken still in the Instant Pot®, use two forks and pull the chicken apart; mix with juices in the Instant Pot®.

4 To assemble the wraps, use a slotted spoon to place ⅛ of the chicken mixture on each tortilla. Top each tortilla with ⅛ cup celery, and 1 tablespoon dressing. Fold the wraps and serve.

BBQ Chicken Legs

What is better than a three-ingredient recipe that cooks in 15 minutes? This amazing recipe will make you realize that the answer is, "Not much!" These super simple, delicious chicken legs are incredibly tender and juicy and are sure to become favorites for your family and friends. Change up this recipe by alternating the hundreds of the barbecue sauce options available.

- **Hands-On Time: 10 minutes**
- **Cook Time: 15 minutes**

Serves 5

1 cup chicken broth
3 pounds (about 10) chicken legs/drumsticks
¾ cup barbecue sauce

INSTANT POT® OPTIONS
If you like your chicken a little crispy, place cooked chicken on a parchment-paper-lined baking sheet and broil for approximately 2 minutes per side.

1 Insert trivet into Instant Pot®. Add chicken broth. Arrange chicken standing up, meaty-side down, on the trivet. Lock lid.

2 Press the Poultry button and cook for the default time of 15 minutes. When timer beeps, let pressure release naturally for 10 minutes. Quick-release any additional pressure until float valve drops and then unlock lid. Check the chicken using a meat thermometer to ensure the internal temperature is at least 165°F.

3 Remove chicken from pot. In a large bowl, gently toss chicken legs in the barbecue sauce and serve.

Thai Chicken Thighs

PALEO, GLUTEN-FREE

Featuring the smoothness of the coconut, the zest from the lime, the heat from the sriracha, and the touch of sweetness from the honey, this chicken is completely balanced in flavor. And don't overlook the sauce. It is so delicious that you may want to use some of it from the pot and ladle it over some steamed and spiraled veggie noodles.

- **Hands-On Time: 10 minutes**
- **Cook Time: 15 minutes**

Serves 5

3 pounds (about 10) chicken legs
1 teaspoon fine sea salt
½ cup canned coconut milk
½ cup chicken broth
2 tablespoons coconut aminos
1 tablespoon tomato paste
1 tablespoon honey
1 teaspoon lime zest
1 tablespoon fresh lime juice
1 tablespoon sriracha
3 cloves garlic, minced
½" knob of gingerroot, peeled and grated
¼ cup chopped fresh cilantro

1 Pat chicken legs dry with a paper towel. On a plate, season chicken with salt. Place in the Instant Pot®.

2 In a medium bowl, whisk together remaining ingredients. Pour mixture over chicken. Lock lid.

3 Press the Poultry button and cook for the default time of 15 minutes. When timer beeps, let pressure release naturally for 10 minutes. Quick-release any additional pressure until float valve drops and then unlock lid. Check the chicken using a meat thermometer to ensure the internal temperature is at least 165°F.

4 Remove chicken from pot, transfer to a platter, and serve warm.

Chicken Chardonnay

If you need an excuse to buy a bottle of wine, this recipe is for you. Drink a glass, share a glass, and then use a glass in this elegant chicken dish that's complete with traditional Italian spices.

- **Hands-On Time: 10 minutes**
- **Cook Time: 20 minutes**

Serves 6

3 pounds chicken breasts, cut into 1" cubes

1 teaspoon fine sea salt

1 teaspoon ground black pepper

3 tablespoons olive oil

1 clove garlic, crushed

1 cup chardonnay

1 (15-ounce) can diced tomatoes, including juice

1 cup sliced mushrooms

1 teaspoon dried thyme

1 teaspoon dried oregano

1 On a plate, rub chicken pieces with salt and pepper.

2 Press the Sauté button on Instant Pot®. Heat the oil and add garlic. Sauté for 1 minute or less, just enough to release the garlic's aroma without burning it. Pour wine and tomatoes into the Instant Pot®. Press the Adjust button to change the temperature to Less and simmer unlidded for 5 minutes.

3 Arrange chicken in a single layer on top of tomato mixture in the Instant Pot®. Add the mushrooms in an even layer. Sprinkle Instant Pot® mixture with thyme and oregano. Lock lid.

4 Press the Manual button and adjust time to 10 minutes. When timer beeps, let pressure release naturally for 10 minutes. Quick-release any additional pressure until float valve drops and then unlock lid. Check the chicken using a meat thermometer to ensure the internal temperature is at least 165°F.

5 Using a slotted spoon, transfer chicken to a serving platter. Press the Sauté button, press the Adjust button to change the temperature to Less, and simmer sauce in Instant Pot® for 5 minutes to thicken. Pour some of the sauce over chicken. Serve warm.

Beer Can Chicken Dijon

Traditionally, a "beer can chicken" dish utilizes a beer can placed in the cavity of a chicken that is then grilled or baked. The purpose is to utilize the steamed flavor from the beer. In this Instant Pot® twist, the flavor is distributed while the beer steams around the chicken. Change up the beer variety for a different flavor experience each time.

- **Hands-On Time: 10 minutes**
- **Cook Time: 20 minutes**

Serves 5

¼ cup Dijon mustard

3 pounds (about 10) chicken legs/drumsticks

1 large onion, peeled and chopped

1 (12-ounce) bottle beer, any brand/variety

INSTANT POT® OPTIONS

A standard can of beer is perfect for the recipe. However, the craft beer market has exploded in recent years and this recipe can be altered for the season. There is pumpkin beer for Fall, stout beer for St. Patty's Day, chocolate beer for Valentine's Day, and a nice pale lager for, well, the rest of the year!

1 Rub Dijon mustard over the chicken legs.

2 Scatter onion in Instant Pot®. Insert trivet. Add beer. Press the Sauté button and simmer unlidded for 5 minutes (press the Adjust button to change the temperature to Less if mixture starts to boil too vigorously). Arrange chicken standing up, meaty-side down, on the trivet. Lock lid.

3 Press the Poultry button and cook for the default time of 15 minutes. When timer beeps, let pressure release naturally for 10 minutes. Quick-release any additional pressure until float valve drops and then unlock lid. Check the chicken using a meat thermometer to ensure the internal temperature is at least 165°F.

4 Remove chicken from pot and serve.

Citrus-Spiced Chicken

PALEO, GLUTEN-FREE

This ridiculously delicious and juicy chicken is spiced just right with a balanced combination of paprika, cinnamon, ginger, nutmeg, and more. Serve with a plate of steamed vegetables or even add a scoop of rice to make this a full meal.

- **Hands-On Time: 15 minutes**
- **Cook Time: 15 minutes**

Serves 8

2 tablespoons olive oil

3 pounds boneless, skinless chicken thighs

1 teaspoon smoked paprika

½ teaspoon sea salt

⅛ teaspoon ground cinnamon

⅛ teaspoon ground ginger

⅛ teaspoon ground nutmeg

½ cup white raisins

½ cup slivered almonds

1 cup freshly squeezed orange juice

⅛ cup freshly squeezed lemon juice

⅛ cup freshly squeezed lime juice

1 pound carrots, peeled and diced large

2 tablespoons water

1 tablespoon arrowroot powder

1 Press the Sauté button on Instant Pot®. Heat olive oil and fry chicken thighs for 2 minutes on each side until browned.

2 Add the paprika, salt, cinnamon, ginger, nutmeg, raisins, almonds, orange juice, lemon juice, lime juice, and carrots. Lock lid.

3 Press the Manual button and adjust time to 10 minutes. When timer beeps, let pressure release naturally for 5 minutes. Quick-release any additional pressure until the float valve drops and then unlock lid. Check the chicken using a meat thermometer to make sure the internal temperature is at least 165°F.

4 Use a slotted spoon to remove chicken, carrots, and raisins and transfer to a serving platter.

5 In a small bowl, whisk together water and arrowroot to create a slurry. Add to liquid in the Instant Pot® and stir to combine. Press Sauté button on Instant Pot®, press Adjust button to change the temperature to Less, and simmer unlidded for 3 minutes until sauce is thickened. Pour sauce over chicken and serve.

Lemongrass Chicken

Fresh lemongrass can be found at most health-food grocers, and specialty Asian food stores will stock it as well. Peel off the hard outer layers to get to the soft core. Most chefs will crush the lemongrass with the side of a knife or hit it a few times on the counter to help release that lemony perfume found in lemongrass.

- **Hands-On Time: 10 minutes**
- **Cook Time: 10 minutes**

Serves 8

1 tablespoon fish sauce

1 tablespoon soy sauce

⅛ cup freshly squeezed lime juice

1 tablespoon honey

½ teaspoon sea salt

¼ teaspoon ground turmeric

⅛ teaspoon red pepper flakes

¼ cup minced lemongrass, tough layers removed

3 pounds boneless, skinless chicken thighs

1 cup chicken broth

¼ cup chopped fresh cilantro

1 In a large bowl, whisk together fish sauce, soy sauce, lime juice, honey, salt, turmeric, red pepper flakes, and lemongrass. Toss chicken in sauce and refrigerate covered for 1 hour.

2 Place trivet in Instant Pot®. Pour in chicken broth. Arrange chicken on a steamer basket and lower onto the trivet. Lock lid.

3 Press the Manual button and adjust time to 10 minutes. When timer beeps, let pressure release naturally for 10 minutes. Quick-release any additional pressure until the float valve drops and then unlock lid. Check the chicken using a meat thermometer to ensure the internal temperature is at least 165°F.

4 Using a slotted spoon, transfer chicken to a serving tray. Garnish with chopped cilantro.

Bourbon Barbecue Chicken

If you like barbecue, you're going to love this Bourbon Barbecue Chicken and the extra kick of sweetness the bourbon brings to the table. Whether you're whipping this dish up for game day or just a simple weeknight meal, you'll leave your guests and family wanting more.

- **Hands-On Time: 10 minutes**
- **Cook Time: 15 minutes**

Serves 5

¼ cup bourbon whiskey

¼ cup pure maple syrup

1 tablespoon Dijon mustard

1 cup ketchup

1 teaspoon garlic powder

1 teaspoon onion salt

1 teaspoon smoked paprika

3 pounds (about 10) chicken legs

1 cup water

1 In a small bowl, whisk together bourbon, maple syrup, mustard, ketchup, garlic powder, onion salt, and smoked paprika. Place chicken in large zip-top bag and pour mixture (reserving 2 tablespoons) over chicken; seal bag and refrigerate for 1 hour.

2 Insert trivet into Instant Pot®. Add water. Arrange chicken standing up, meaty-side down, on the trivet. Lock lid.

3 Press the Poultry button and cook for the default time of 15 minutes. When timer beeps, let pressure release naturally for 10 minutes. Quick-release any additional pressure until the float valve drops and then unlock lid. Check the chicken using a meat thermometer to ensure the internal temperature is at least 165°F.

4 Transfer chicken to a serving tray. Brush with remaining 2 tablespoons sauce and serve.

Coconut Curry Chicken

PALEO, GLUTEN-FREE

Thai-influenced dishes have historically been very spicy to the American palette. This recipe has downplayed the heat level to accommodate those taste buds. But if you can handle it, take the sriracha up a notch and go crazy! When making this recipe, use the full-fat canned version of coconut milk. The refrigerated version is more processed and thinner than the canned counterpart, which is less healthy and will render a thinner sauce.

- **Hands-On Time: 10 minutes**
- **Cook Time: 10 minutes**

Serves 8

1 (14-ounce) can coconut
    milk
1 tablespoon red curry paste
1 tablespoon lime juice
1 teaspoon lime zest
1 teaspoon sea salt
1 teaspoon white pepper
1 teaspoon ground turmeric
1 tablespoon sriracha
3 pounds boneless, skinless
    chicken thighs
1 cup chicken broth
¼ cup chopped fresh cilantro

1   In a medium bowl, whisk together coconut milk, red curry paste, lime juice, lime zest, salt, pepper, turmeric, and sriracha. Place chicken in a large zip-top bag and pour mixture over chicken. Seal bag and toss to coat. Refrigerate for 1 hour.

2   Place trivet in Instant Pot®. Pour in chicken broth. Arrange chicken on a steamer basket and lower onto trivet. Lock lid.

3   Press the Manual button and adjust time to 10 minutes. When timer beeps, let pressure release naturally for 10 minutes. Quick-release any additional pressure until the float valve drops and then unlock lid. Check the chicken using a meat thermometer to ensure the internal temperature is at least 165°F.

4   Using a slotted spoon, transfer chicken to a serving tray. Garnish with chopped cilantro and serve.

Beef and Pork Main Dishes

There is nothing better suited for the Instant Pot® than meat. The steam and pressure can take a seemingly tough piece of meat and make it taste like butter in your mouth. The steam keeps everything moist, and the pressure helps break down some of the sinewy parts. And the best part? The trapped steam helps create a meat that tastes like it has been braised for hours in about 30 minutes, depending on the weight. In addition, you can add your potatoes and other vegetables to the pot while cooking. Not only will you have a complete meal, but the vegetables take on a completely new savory flavor by cooking next to the meat. With recipes ranging from Tipsy Chuck Roast and Hawaiian Pulled Pork to Mongolian Beef BBQ and Korean Short Ribs, this chapter will help get you started on some classic Instant Pot® recipes.

Hawaiian Pulled Pork

This island-inspired pulled pork is fantastic on its own or when served on slider buns, flour tortillas, or lettuce wraps. For even more flavor, add avocado slices, grated cheese, sliced radishes, or sour cream. The recipe may look like it contains a lot of ingredients, but don't be intimidated. You probably have most of these spices already on your spice rack.

- **Hands-On Time: 15 minutes**
- **Cook Time: 95 minutes**

Serves 10

1 (5-pound) bone-in pork butt or shoulder

Dry Rub
½ teaspoon ground ginger
½ teaspoon celery seed
½ teaspoon cayenne pepper
1 teaspoon garlic powder
1 teaspoon sea salt
1 teaspoon onion powder
1 teaspoon ground cumin

Sauce
1 (8-ounce) can crushed pineapple
¼ cup soy sauce
¼ cup tomato sauce
¼ cup pure maple syrup
1 tablespoon rice wine
3 cloves garlic, peeled and halved
1 tablespoon grated fresh ginger

1 Dry pork butt with paper towels and set aside.

2 **For Dry Rub:** In a small bowl, combine Dry Rub ingredients. Massage rub into all sides of the pork. Refrigerate covered for 1 hour up to overnight.

3 **For Sauce:** Combine Sauce ingredients in a small saucepan. Bring to a boil. Reduce heat and simmer for 10 minutes until sauce reduces by a quarter and starts to thicken. Let cool for 5 minutes. Add to a food processor and pulse until smooth.

4 Place the pork butt in the Instant Pot® and pour the sauce over the meat. Lock lid.

5 Press the Manual button and adjust time to 85 minutes. When timer beeps, let the pressure release naturally until float valve drops and then unlock lid. Check the pork to make sure it can easily pull apart. If not, press the Sauté button and simmer unlidded for an additional 10 minutes.

6 With the meat still in the Instant Pot®, use two forks and pull pork apart. Remove bone and discard. Stir pork with sauce in the Instant Pot®. Serve using a slotted spoon.

Make-Ahead Steps

Both the Dry Rub and the Sauce can be made ahead of time. A weekly prep day is essential for a busy schedule during the week. It helps keep you on track and away from those highly processed drive-thru meals.

Tipsy Chuck Roast

Although the dark lager used in this recipe lends an incredibly rich flavor, you can and should feel free to change this recipe to suit your personal tastes. If you'd prefer, try using one of the many gluten-free beers available. If cooking with alcohol isn't your thing, beef broth with a dash of Worcestershire sauce will do the trick nicely.

- **Hands-On Time: 15 minutes**
- **Cook Time: 65 minutes**

Serves 8

2 tablespoons Dijon mustard

1 teaspoon sea salt

½ teaspoon ground black pepper

1 teaspoon smoked paprika

1 (3-pound) boneless chuck roast

1 tablespoon olive oil

1 (12-ounce) bottle dark lager

2 tablespoons tomato paste

1 cup beef broth

2 teaspoons Worcestershire sauce

1 medium yellow onion, peeled and diced

2 large carrots, peeled and diced

1 small stalk celery, diced

2 cups sliced mushrooms

1 In a small bowl, combine the mustard, salt, pepper, and paprika. Cover all sides of the meat with the mustard mixture.

2 Press the Sauté button. Heat oil. Sear meat on all sides, about 5 minutes. Remove the meat and set aside.

3 Add beer and deglaze the Instant Pot® by stirring and scraping bottom and sides of Instant Pot® to loosen any browned bits.

4 Whisk in the tomato paste. Add the meat back into the pot along with the broth, Worcestershire sauce, onion, carrots, celery, and mushrooms. Lock lid.

5 Press the Manual button and adjust time to 60 minutes. When timer beeps, let pressure release naturally until float valve drops and then unlock lid.

6 Remove the meat to a serving platter. Let rest for 5 minutes. Slice. If desired, use an immersion blender to purée the juices in the Instant Pot®. Pour juices over the sliced meat. Serve warm.

INSTANT POT® OPTIONS

This is a dish where you can have fun with the many flavors and types of mustard available today. Dijon is a fan favorite, but horseradish mustard is another excellent pairing with beef dishes. Branch out and explore.

Barbecue Flank Steak Taco Filling

This is a mix of a few worlds that come together beautifully. Let's call it Memphis Tex-Mex! A little barbecue flavor goes a long way into spicing up your flank steak. What a great addition to your Taco Tuesday tradition whether served on lettuce leaves, tortillas, or taco shells.

- **Hands-On Time: 10 minutes**
- **Cook Time: 45 minutes**

Serves 4

¼ cup ketchup

¼ cup apricot preserves

⅛ cup honey

⅛ cup apple cider vinegar

¼ cup soy sauce

⅛ teaspoon cayenne pepper

1 teaspoon ground mustard

¼ teaspoon ground black pepper

1 (2-pound) flank steak

2 tablespoons avocado oil, divided

1 large sweet onion, peeled and sliced

1½ cups beef broth

INSTANT POT® OPTIONS

For your family members or guests who are gluten-intolerant or don't prefer tortillas, put out a plate of lettuce leaves for another choice of wraps. Although iceberg lettuce is a great alternative and gives a bit of crunch, Bibb lettuce works well, too, easily contouring to the filling.

1 In a small bowl, combine ketchup, preserves, honey, vinegar, soy sauce, cayenne pepper, mustard, and pepper. Spread mixture on all sides of the flank steak.

2 Press the Sauté button on Instant Pot®. Heat 1 tablespoon oil. Sear meat on each side for approximately 5 minutes. Remove the meat and set aside. Add remaining 1 tablespoon oil and onions. Sauté onions for 3–5 minutes until translucent.

3 Add beef broth. Set meat and all of the sauce on the layer of onions. Lock lid.

4 Press the Meat button and adjust time to 35 minutes. When timer beeps, let pressure release naturally until float valve drops and then unlock lid.

5 Transfer the meat to a serving platter. Thinly slice against the grain and serve immediately.

Pork Chops and Sauerkraut

These pork chops are juicy and flavorful with a German flair from the addition of beer, potatoes, sauerkraut, and caraway seeds. If you're looking for a nonalcoholic option, feel free to substitute beef broth for the beer.

- **Hands-On Time: 15 minutes**
- **Cook Time: 30 minutes**

Serves 4

2 tablespoons olive oil

4 (1"-thick) bone-in pork loin chops

1 teaspoon sea salt

½ teaspoon ground black pepper

4 slices bacon, diced

1 stalk celery, finely chopped

3 large carrots, peeled and sliced

1 large onion, peeled and diced

1 clove garlic, peeled and minced

1 (12-ounce) bottle lager

4 medium red potatoes, peeled and quartered

2 medium red apples, peeled, cored, and quartered

1 (1-pound) bag high-quality sauerkraut, rinsed and drained

1 tablespoon caraway seeds

1 Press the Sauté button on Instant Pot®. Heat olive oil. Season pork chops with salt and pepper. In batches, sear pork chops for 1–2 minutes per side. Set pork aside.

2 Add bacon, celery, carrots, and onion to the Instant Pot®. Stir-fry for 3–5 minutes until the onions are translucent. Add garlic and cook for another minute. Add beer and deglaze the Instant Pot® by stirring and scraping to loosen any browned bits stuck to the bottom and sides of the Instant Pot®. Simmer unlidded for 5 minutes.

3 Add potatoes, apples, and sauerkraut. Sprinkle with caraway seeds. Slightly prop pork chops up against the sides of the pot so as not to crowd the pork. Lock lid.

4 Press the Manual button and adjust time to 15 minutes. When timer beeps, let pressure release naturally for 5 minutes. Quick-release any additional pressure until float valve drops and then unlock lid.

5 Transfer the pork chops, sauerkraut, potatoes, and apples to a serving tray.

Steak Fajitas

PALEO, GLUTEN-FREE

This simple dish with such depth of flavor can be enjoyed for dinner, lunch, or even for breakfast as most paleo folks like their leftover meat in the morning, served with a side of scrambled eggs and a thick slice of avocado. There are so many ways to enjoy this tasty beef so dive on in!

- **Hands-On Time: 15 minutes**
- **Cook Time: 45 minutes**

Serves 6

⅛ cup avocado oil
¼ cup coconut aminos
1 tablespoon fish sauce
1 teaspoon ground cumin
1 teaspoon chili powder
2 tablespoons tomato paste
½ teaspoon sea salt
1 (2-pound) skirt steak
1 small onion, peeled and diced
1 medium green bell pepper, seeded and diced
1 medium red bell pepper, seeded and diced
1 cup beef broth

INSTANT POT® OPTIONS
Iceberg and Bibb lettuce are two great choices for lettuce wraps if you'd like to wrap up your fajitas. And feel free to take this dish up a notch by adding julienned radishes, fresh cilantro, avocado slices, and even diced tomatoes.

1   In a small bowl, combine oil, coconut aminos, fish sauce, cumin, chili powder, tomato paste, and salt. Spread ¾ of the mixture on all sides of the beef. Reserve additional sauce.

2   Press the Sauté button on Instant Pot®. Add skirt steak and sear on each side for approximately 5 minutes. Remove the meat and set aside. Add onion and peppers to Instant Pot® with reserved sauce. Sauté for 3–5 minutes until onions are translucent.

3   Add beef broth. Set meat on the layer of onion and peppers. Lock lid.

4   Press the Meat button and cook for the default time of 35 minutes. When timer beeps, let the pressure release naturally until float valve drops and then unlock lid.

5   Using a slotted spoon, remove the meat and vegetables to a serving platter. Thinly slice the skirt steak against the grain. Serve.

Cowboy Baby Back Ribs

These Instant Pot® ribs are amazingly juicy due to the pressure and constant steam in the pot. Don't skip the coffee crystals with this rustically charming recipe. It adds a beautiful earthiness to the ribs. If you want a little caramelization to the ribs, throw them on the grill or under a broiler for a couple of minutes until browned on each side.

- **Hands-On Time: 40 minutes**
- **Cook Time: 30 minutes**

Serves 6

2 racks (about 3 pounds) baby back pork ribs
1 teaspoon instant coffee crystals
1 teaspoon sea salt
½ teaspoon chili powder
½ teaspoon ground cumin
½ teaspoon cayenne pepper
½ teaspoon ground mustard
½ teaspoon garlic powder
½ teaspoon onion powder
¼ teaspoon ground coriander
¼ cup pure maple syrup
¼ cup soy sauce
1 tablespoon apple cider vinegar
2 tablespoons tomato paste
1 tablespoon olive oil
1 medium onion, peeled and large diced

1 Cut ribs into 2-rib sections. In a small bowl, combine coffee, salt, chili powder, cumin, cayenne pepper, mustard, garlic powder, onion powder, and coriander. Using your hands, rub this mixture into the rib sections. Refrigerate covered for 30 minutes up to overnight.

2 In a small mixing bowl, whisk together maple syrup, soy sauce, apple cider vinegar, and tomato paste.

3 Press the Sauté button on Instant Pot®. Heat olive oil. Add onions and sauté for 3–5 minutes until onions are translucent. Add the maple syrup mixture. Using tongs, add a few ribs at a time and gently coat them in sauce. Arrange ribs standing upright with the meaty side facing outward. Lock lid.

4 Press the Manual button and adjust time to 25 minutes. When the timer beeps, let pressure release naturally until float valve drops and then unlock lid. Serve warm.

Korean Short Ribs

Short ribs are just that: ribs taken from the short portion of the rib bone of cattle. There are two types of cuts with short ribs: flanken and English cut. For this recipe, flanken is the preferred choice. Your butcher can help achieve this if there are no prepackaged options. Otherwise, the sauce of this recipe will work to flavor any cut of meat you prefer.

- **Hands-On Time: 10 minutes**
- **Cook Time: 25 minutes**

Serves 6

½ cup soy sauce
½ cup pure maple syrup
½ cup rice wine
1 tablespoon sesame oil
1 teaspoon white pepper
½ teaspoon ground ginger
½ teaspoon garlic powder
½ teaspoon gochujang
3 pounds beef short ribs
1 cup beef broth
2 green onions, sliced
1 tablespoon toasted sesame seeds

1 In a small bowl, combine soy sauce, maple syrup, rice wine, sesame oil, white pepper, ground ginger, garlic powder, and gochujang. Using your hands, rub this mixture into the rib sections. Refrigerate covered for 60 minutes up to overnight.

2 Add beef broth to Instant Pot®. Insert trivet. Arrange ribs standing upright with the meaty side facing outward. Lock lid.

3 Press the Manual button and adjust time to 25 minutes. When the timer beeps, let pressure release naturally until float valve drops and then unlock lid.

4 Transfer ribs to a serving platter and garnish with green onions and sesame seeds.

What Is Gochujang?

Gochujang is a fermented Korean spicy condiment made from red chilies, rice, and soybeans. It can be found in high-end grocers as well as local Asian stores. The more readily available Thai red chili paste can used instead of gochujang in this recipe.

Balsamic Pork Chops with Figs and Pears

PALEO, GLUTEN-FREE

The flavors in this recipe are so sophisticated that your guests will never know you took less than 30 minutes to whip up this juicy masterpiece. Figs—a superfood high in potassium and fiber—are one of those underused fruits that pair so nicely with pork chops and a good wine that you may never pay for fine dining again.

- **Hands-On Time: 10 minutes**
- **Cook Time: 15 minutes**

Serves 2

2 (1"-thick) bone-in pork chops
1 teaspoon sea salt
1 teaspoon ground black pepper
¼ cup balsamic vinegar
¼ cup chicken broth
1 tablespoon dried mint
2 tablespoons avocado oil
1 medium sweet onion, peeled and sliced
3 pears, peeled, cored, and diced large
5 dried figs, stems removed and halved

1 Pat the pork chops dry with a paper towel and season both sides liberally with salt and pepper. Set aside.

2 In a small bowl, whisk together vinegar, broth, and mint. Set aside.

3 Press the Sauté button on the Instant Pot®. Heat oil. Brown pork chops for 5 minutes per side. Remove chops and set aside.

4 Add vinegar mixture and deglaze the Instant Pot® by scraping the brown bits from the sides and bottom of the Instant Pot®. Layer the onions into the pot, then scatter the pears and figs over onions. Place pork chops on top. Lock lid.

5 Press the Steam button and adjust time to 3 minutes. When the timer beeps, let pressure release naturally for 10 minutes. Quick-release any additional pressure until the float valve drops and then unlock lid.

6 Using a slotted spoon, transfer pork, onions, figs, and pears to a serving platter. Serve warm.

Quick and Easy Meatloaf

Meatloaf is a worldwide tradition. It seems that every country in the world has a variation on this simple dish. As long as you have some form of ground meat, vegetables, and a binding agent, a meatloaf can be made. This Quick and Easy Meatloaf is the perfect weeknight staple, especially when served with potatoes and vegetables.

- **Hands-On Time: 10 minutes**
- **Cook Time: 35 minutes**

Serves 6

1 pound ground beef
1 pound ground pork
4 large eggs
1 cup panko bread crumbs
1 large shallot, finely diced
¼ cup seeded and finely diced red bell pepper
½ cup tomato sauce
1 tablespoon Italian seasoning
½ teaspoon smoked paprika
½ teaspoon garlic powder
½ teaspoon celery seed
1 teaspoon sea salt
½ teaspoon ground black pepper
1 cup beef broth

1 Using your hands, in a large bowl combine all ingredients except the broth.

2 Form mixture into a ball, flatten the top, then place meatloaf into a 7-cup glass dish.

3 Add beef broth to the Instant Pot®. Insert trivet. Place glass dish on top of the trivet. Lock lid.

4 Press the Meat button and cook for the default time of 35 minutes. When timer beeps, let pressure release naturally for 10 minutes. Quick-release any additional pressure until float valve drops and then unlock lid.

5 Remove meatloaf from Instant Pot® and let cool at room temperature for 10 minutes. Tilt glass bowl over the sink and pour out any liquid/rendered fat. Slice and serve.

Utensil Hacks

You may want to fashion an aluminum foil sling for easy retrieval if you don't have a pair of plate retriever tongs. Take an approximate 10" × 10" square of aluminum foil and fold it back and forth until you have a 2" × 10" sling. Place sling under the bowl or pan before cooking so that you can easily lift up the heated dish when cooking is complete.

Cherry-Rosemary Pork Tenderloin

Pork tenderloin is easy to overcook and dry out, but the steaming nature of the Instant Pot® creates a nice, tender loin of pork. To make this dish look as amazing as it tastes, top with additional cherry preserves and garnish with sprigs of fresh rosemary (just be sure to avoid eating the rosemary!). You're guaranteed to have a company-worthy meal that won't stress you out while preparing.

- **Hands-On Time: 5 minutes**
- **Cook Time: 30 minutes**

Serves 6

2 tablespoons avocado oil

2 (3-pound) pork tenderloins, halved

½ cup balsamic vinegar

¼ cup olive oil

¼ cup cherry preserves

½ teaspoon sea salt

¼ teaspoon ground black pepper

¼ cup finely chopped fresh rosemary

4 garlic cloves, minced

1 Press the Sauté button on the Instant Pot®. Heat oil. Brown pork on all sides, about 2 minutes per side (4 sides total).

2 In a small bowl, whisk remaining ingredients together and pour over the pork. Lock lid.

3 Press the Manual button and adjust time to 20 minutes. When timer beeps, let the pressure release naturally for 5 minutes. Quick-release any additional pressure until float valve drops and then unlock lid.

4 Transfer tenderloin to a cutting board. Let rest for 5 minutes. Slice into medallions and serve.

INSTANT POT® OPTIONS

Do you have some fresh cherries you need to use? Instead of the cherry preserves, try this Quick Homemade Cherry Coulis. Place about ¼ cup pitted and quartered cherries, ¼ cup water, and ¼ cup pure maple syrup in a small saucepan. Bring to a boil, simmer for 10 minutes until reduced by half, then "smoosh" the cherries against the side of the pan. Let cool and use this in place of the preserves.

Carnitas Lettuce Wraps

PALEO, GLUTEN-FREE

When you think of cooking a pork shoulder, you probably think about cooking it low and slow for 6–8 hours. With the Instant Pot®, the same result can be achieved in a significantly reduced time. Enjoy this succulent meat topped with fresh jalapeño, radishes, avocado, and tomatoes . . . all wrapped neatly in a fresh lettuce leaf!

- **Hands-On Time: 10 minutes**
- **Cook Time: 60 minutes**

Serves 6

1 tablespoon unsweetened cocoa powder
2 teaspoons salt
1 teaspoon cayenne pepper
2 teaspoons ground oregano
1 teaspoon white pepper
1 teaspoon garlic powder
1 teaspoon onion salt
1 teaspoon ground cumin
½ teaspoon ground coriander
1 (3-pound) pork shoulder
2 tablespoons olive oil
2–3 cups water
1 head butter lettuce, washed and dried
1 small jalapeño, sliced
¼ cup julienned radishes
1 medium avocado, diced
2 small Roma tomatoes, diced
2 limes, cut into wedges

1. In a small bowl, combine cocoa powder, salt, cayenne pepper, oregano, white pepper, garlic powder, onion salt, cumin, and coriander. Massage seasoning into pork shoulder and refrigerate covered overnight.

2. Press the Sauté button on the Instant Pot®. Add 2 tablespoons oil. Sear roast on all sides ensuring all sides are browned, about 8–10 minutes. Add enough water (2–3 cups) to almost cover the meat. Lock lid.

3. Press the Manual button and adjust time to 45 minutes. When timer beeps, let pressure release naturally for 10 minutes. Quick-release any additional pressure until float valve drops and then unlock lid.

4. Transfer pork to a platter. Using two forks, shred the meat. Discard all but ½ cup of cooking liquid. Add meat back into Instant Pot®. Press the Sauté button and stir-fry meat for 4–5 minutes creating some crispy edges.

5. Serve with lettuce leaves, jalapeño slices, radishes, avocado, tomatoes, and lime wedges.

Italian Sausage and Peppers Hoagies

Stuff these spiced peppers and sausage into a hoagie roll for complete Chi-town happiness! To make it even more authentic, dip your hoagie into the cooking juices before serving, creating the "wet roll" popular in restaurants and street fairs among Chicago residents.

- **Hands-On Time: 15 minutes**
- **Cook Time: 20 minutes**

Serves 6

2 tablespoons olive oil, divided

1 pound sweet Italian sausage links, uncooked, divided

1 large onion, peeled and sliced

1 small red bell pepper, seeded and sliced

1 small green bell pepper, seeded and sliced

1 small yellow bell pepper, seeded and sliced

4 cloves garlic, minced

½ cup chicken broth

1 (15-ounce) can diced stewed tomatoes, including juice

¼ cup chopped fresh basil

2 tablespoons fresh oregano leaves

1 teaspoon cayenne pepper

1 teaspoon sea salt

½ teaspoon ground black pepper

6 hoagie rolls

1 Press the Sauté button on the Instant Pot®. Heat 1 tablespoon olive oil. Add half of the sausage links and brown all sides for about 4–5 minutes. Remove and set aside. Add the remaining 1 tablespoon olive oil and remaining sausages. Brown all sides for another 4–5 minutes. Remove from Instant Pot® and set aside.

2 Add onions and bell peppers to Instant Pot® and stir-fry for 3–5 minutes until onions are translucent. Add garlic. Cook for an additional minute. Add broth and deglaze Instant Pot® by scraping the sides and bottom of the Instant Pot®. Add tomatoes, basil, oregano, cayenne pepper, salt, and pepper. Lock lid.

3 Press the Manual button and adjust time to 5 minutes. When timer beeps, quick-release the pressure until float valve drops and then unlock the lid.

4 Using a slotted spoon, transfer pot ingredients to a serving platter. Slice sausages. Serve on hoagie rolls.

Mama's Meatballs

Everyone loves meatballs, and this tender dish will rival anything your mama ever made! Completely caramelized and made with a delicious mixture of both beef and pork that gives this dish it's unique flavor, these meatballs are ready-made for a delicious family dinner. Serve the meatballs with a nice side salad or on top of rice, pasta, or spiraled vegetables.

- **Hands-On Time: 15 minutes**
- **Cook Time: 30 minutes**

Serves 4

½ **pound ground beef**
½ **pound ground pork**
2 large eggs
**1 tablespoon Italian
    seasoning**
1 teaspoon garlic powder
1 teaspoon celery seed
½ **teaspoon onion powder**
½ **teaspoon smoked paprika**
½ **cup old-fashioned oats**
**2 tablespoons plus 2 cups
    marinara sauce, divided**
**3 tablespoons avocado oil,
    divided**
2 cups water

1 In a medium bowl, combine beef, pork, eggs, Italian seasoning, garlic powder, celery seed, onion powder, smoked paprika, oats, and 2 tablespoons marinara sauce. Form into 20 meatballs. Set aside.

2 Press the Sauté button on the Instant Pot® and heat 2 tablespoons oil. Place 10 meatballs around the edge of the pot. Sear all sides of the meatballs for about 4 minutes. Remove the first batch and set aside. Add another tablespoon of oil and add remaining meatballs and sear them. Remove meatballs.

3 Discard extra juice and oil from the Instant Pot®. Add seared meatballs to a 7-cup glass dish. Top with remaining 2 cups marinara sauce.

4 Add water to the Instant Pot®. Add trivet. Place the glass dish on top of the trivet. Lock lid.

5 Press the Manual button and adjust time to 20 minutes. When the timer beeps, let pressure release naturally for 10 minutes. Quick-release any additional pressure until float valve drops and then unlock lid.

6 Transfer meatballs to a serving dish.

Mongolian Beef BBQ

PALEO, GLUTEN-FREE

This is a dish that can be translated 100 different ways! Typically when you order this dish in restaurants, you go through the line and pick your meat, vegetables, oil, and sauces, and then hand it over to the chef who cooks it right in front of you. So don't be shy about deleting or adding ingredients.

- **Hands-On Time: 15 minutes**
- **Cook Time: 20 minutes**

Serves 4

1 tablespoon sesame oil

1 (2-pound) skirt steak, sliced into thin strips

¼ cup coconut aminos

½ cup pure maple syrup

1" knob of fresh gingerroot, peeled and grated

4 cloves garlic, minced

½ cup plus 2 tablespoons water, divided

2 tablespoons arrowroot powder

INSTANT POT® OPTIONS
Serve this dish with sliced green onions, roasted cashews, or baby corn cut into thirds to create a full meal.

1 Press the Sauté button on the Instant Pot®. Heat oil and cook steak strips until barely seared on all sides, about 2–3 minutes.

2 In a medium bowl, whisk together coconut aminos, maple syrup, ginger, garlic, and ½ cup water. Pour over beef and stir to deglaze any bits around the edges and bottom of the Instant Pot®. Lock lid.

3 Press the Manual button and adjust time to 10 minutes. When timer beeps, quick-release pressure until float valve drops and then unlock lid.

4 In a small dish, whisk together arrowroot and 2 tablespoons water until smooth to create a slurry. Stir this mixture into the beef mixture. Press Sauté button, press Adjust button to change the temperature to Less, and simmer unlidded for 5 minutes until the sauce thickens.

5 Ladle mixture into bowls and serve.

Cubano Sloppy Joe Wraps

These sloppy Joes have all the flavors of a traditional cubano sandwich without any of the hassle. To make this dish paleo-friendly, delete the tortillas and cheese and add a poached egg on top to make up for the gooiness of the eliminated cheese. If you are gluten-free, most grocers carry a gluten-free tortilla. There are many ways to enjoy this flavorful combination, so choose your path and chow down!

- **Hands-On Time: 10 minutes**
- **Cook Time: 10 minutes**

Serves 8

1 pound ground pork
½ medium onion, peeled and diced
¼ cup chicken broth
1 tablespoon fresh lime juice
1 tablespoon fresh orange juice
1 teaspoon garlic powder
1 teaspoon dried oregano
1 teaspoon cayenne pepper
2 teaspoons ground cumin
1 teaspoon sea salt
1 teaspoon ground black pepper
8 slices Swiss cheese
8 (8") flour tortillas
8 slices ham
24 dill pickle slices
8 teaspoons yellow mustard

1 Press the Sauté button on Instant Pot®. Stir-fry the ground pork and onions for 5 minutes until pork is no longer pink.

2 Add chicken broth and deglaze the Instant Pot® by scraping any brown bits from the sides and bottom of the Instant Pot®. Stir in the lime juice, orange juice, garlic powder, oregano, cayenne pepper, cumin, salt, and pepper. Lock lid.

3 Press the Manual button and adjust time to 5 minutes. When timer beeps, let pressure release naturally until float valve drops and then unlock lid.

4 To assemble the tortillas lay a slice of Swiss cheese on a flour tortilla. Add a slice of ham and 3 pickle slices to each tortilla. Spread 1 teaspoon of yellow mustard down the center. Using a slotted spoon, dip ⅛ of the ground pork mixture from the Instant Pot® and add it down the middle. Fold the bottom 2–3" of the tortilla upward and then flip the sides of the tortilla toward the center. Repeat for remaining tortillas. Serve immediately.

Beef Biryani

In this amazing Instant Pot® dish, tender strips of beef are nestled beautifully in a creamy yogurt-based sauce. The warm spices used in this recipe not only make your taste buds dance, but the fragrant aroma will summon everyone toward the kitchen without you ever saying a word. Served over basmati rice, this meal is to die for.

- **Hands-On Time: 10 minutes**
- **Cook Time: 25 minutes**

Serves 6

1 tablespoon ghee

1 small onion, peeled and sliced

1 pound top round, cut into strips

1 tablespoon minced fresh gingerroot

2 cloves garlic, peeled and minced

½ teaspoon ground cloves

½ teaspoon ground cardamom

½ teaspoon ground coriander

½ teaspoon ground black pepper

½ teaspoon ground cinnamon

½ teaspoon ground cumin

1 teaspoon salt

1 cup plain yogurt

1 (28-ounce) can whole stewed tomatoes, including juice

2 cups cooked basmati rice

1 Press the Sauté button on Instant Pot®. Melt ghee. Add onion and sauté for 3–5 minutes until translucent. Add remaining ingredients, except for the rice, to Instant Pot®. Lock lid.

2 Press the Manual button and adjust time to 10 minutes. When timer beeps, quick-release the pressure until float valve drops and then unlock lid.

3 Press Sauté button, press Adjust button and change the temperature to Less, and simmer uncovered for approximately 10 minutes until most of the liquid has evaporated. Serve over cooked basmati rice.

Mexican Stuffed Peppers

Because of the chorizo, these Mexican Stuffed Peppers can be a little spicy. If heat isn't something you enjoy, then just substitute additional pork sausage for the chorizo. You still won't be short on flavor with this south-of-the-border treat.

- **Hands-On Time: 10 minutes**
- **Cook Time: 20 minutes**

Serves 4

4 large red bell peppers
¼ pound chorizo, loose or cut from casings
½ pound ground pork
1 medium onion, peeled and diced
1 small Roma tomato, diced
1 tablespoon tomato paste
½ cup corn kernels (cut from the cob is preferred)
1 large egg
1 teaspoon ground cumin
1 teaspoon sea salt
1 teaspoon garlic powder
½ cup vegetable broth
½ cup shredded Cheddar cheese

1 Cut off the bell pepper tops as close to the tops as possible. Hollow out and discard seeds. Poke a few small holes in the bottom of the peppers to allow the fat drippings to drain.

2 In a medium bowl, combine remaining ingredients except for broth and cheese. Stuff equal amounts of mixture into each of the bell peppers.

3 Place trivet into the Instant Pot® and pour in the broth. Set the peppers upright on the trivet. Lock lid.

4 Press the Manual button and adjust time to 15 minutes. When the timer beeps, let the pressure release naturally until float valve drops and then unlock lid. Top each pepper with cheese, press Sauté button on Instant Pot®, press Adjust button and change temperature to Less, and simmer for 3 minutes until cheese melts.

5 Transfer peppers to a platter and serve warm.

Swiss Steak and Potatoes

This Swiss Steak and Potatoes recipe is comfort food at its finest. Quick, cheap, and easy are three words that speak to a busy person. By making this succulent dish in the Instant Pot®, the pieces of beef, rich gravy, and seasoned diced potatoes will be in your belly in less than 1 hour.

- **Hands-On Time: 10 minutes**
- **Cook Time: 35 minutes**

Serves 6

2½ (1"-thick) pounds beef round steak

1 teaspoon sea salt

½ teaspoon ground black pepper

2 tablespoons olive oil, divided

1 medium yellow onion, peeled and diced

2 stalks celery, diced

1 large green bell pepper, seeded and diced

1 cup tomato juice

1 cup beef broth

6 large carrots, peeled and cut into 1" pieces

6 medium Yukon gold potatoes, diced large

4 teaspoons butter

1 Cut the round steak into 6 serving-sized pieces and season both sides with salt and pepper.

2 Press the Sauté button on the Instant Pot®. Heat 1 tablespoon oil. Add 3 pieces of meat and sear for 3 minutes on each side. Move to a platter and repeat with the remaining 1 tablespoon oil and the other 3 pieces of meat.

3 Leave the last 3 pieces of browned meat in the Instant Pot®; add the onion, celery, and green pepper on top of them. Lay in the other 3 pieces of meat and pour the tomato juice and broth over them. Place the carrots and potatoes on top of the meat. Lock lid.

4 Press the Manual button and adjust time to 20 minutes. When timer beeps, quick-release pressure until float valve drops and then unlock lid.

5 Transfer the potatoes, carrots, and meat to a serving platter. Cover and keep warm.

6 Skim any fat from the juices remaining in the Instant Pot®. Press the Sauté button on the Instant Pot®, press Adjust button and change temperature to Less, and simmer the juices unlidded for 5 minutes.

7 Whisk in the butter 1 teaspoon at a time. Serve the resulting gravy available at the table to pour over the meat. Serve immediately.

9

Seafood and Fish Main Dishes

Seafood often gets ordered out at restaurants but is overlooked at home. And that's a shame, because fish is not only low in calories and full of nutrients, but is one of the quickest meals you can cook in your Instant Pot®.

The first step to cooking delicious seafood is to trust where you're buying your fresh seafood or to purchase a sealed, frozen product. If you're working with a fishmonger, don't be afraid to ask when the shipment came in, where it came from, was it wild-caught, and can they prepare the fish for you? If that fishmonger can't or won't answer those questions, find another one.

Once you've selected your fish, prepare your meal within 1–2 days for optimal freshness. Also, remember to use the Instant Pot®'s quick-release feature for the dishes in this chapter, which range from Coconut Curry Sea Bass to Low-Country Boil. You don't want to do a natural release with most fish, as it will continue to cook and become dried out if the pressure releases slowly.

Pistachio-Crusted Halibut

The pistachios that encrust this dish give this fish a unique flavor. Pistachios have a rich and nutty flavor and add a distinct texture to the sweetness of the halibut.

- **Hands-On Time: 5 minutes**
- **Cook Time: 7 minutes**

Serves 2

1 tablespoon Dijon mustard
1 teaspoon fresh lemon juice
2 tablespoons panko bread crumbs
¼ cup chopped unsalted pistachios
½ teaspoon salt
2 (5-ounce) halibut fillets
1 cup water

1 Preheat the oven to broiler for 500°F.

2 In a small bowl, combine mustard, lemon juice, bread crumbs, pistachios, and salt to form a thick paste.

3 Pat the halibut fillets dry with a paper towel. Rub the paste on the top of each fillet and place in steamer basket.

4 Pour 1 cup water in the Instant Pot®. Insert trivet. Place steamer basket on trivet. Lock lid.

5 Press the Manual button and adjust time to 5 minutes. When timer beeps, quick-release the pressure until float valve drops and then unlock lid. Transfer fillets to a parchment-paper-lined baking sheet.

6 Broil for approximately 1–2 minutes until tops are browned. Remove from heat and serve hot.

Trout in Herb Sauce

If the trout haven't already been gutted, your fishmonger will be happy to do this for you. All you have to do is ask! Once home use your fish within 1–2 days with this incredibly creamy and fresh traditional herb sauce.

- **Hands-On Time: 5 minutes**
- **Cook Time: 5 minutes**

Serves 4

Trout

4 (½-pound) fresh river trout

1 teaspoon sea salt

4 cups torn lettuce leaves, divided

1 teaspoon white wine vinegar

½ cup water

Herb Sauce

½ cup minced fresh flat-leaf parsley

2 teaspoons Italian seasoning

1 small shallot, peeled and minced

2 tablespoons mayonnaise

½ teaspoon fresh lemon juice

¼ teaspoon sugar

Pinch of salt

2 tablespoons sliced almonds, toasted

1 **For Trout:** Rinse the trout inside and out; pat dry. Sprinkle with salt inside and out. Put 3 cups lettuce leaves in the bottom of the Instant Pot®. Arrange the trout over the top of the lettuce and top fish with the remaining lettuce.

2 Pour vinegar and water into pot. Lock lid.

3 Press the Manual button and adjust time to 3 minutes. When the timer beeps, let pressure release naturally for 3 minutes. Quick-release any additional pressure until float valve drops and then unlock lid.

4 Transfer fish to a serving plate. Peel and discard the skin from the fish. Remove and discard the heads if desired.

5 **For Herb Sauce:** In a small bowl, mix together the parsley, Italian seasoning, shallot, mayonnaise, lemon juice, sugar, and salt. Evenly divide among the fish, spreading it over them. Sprinkle toasted almonds over the top of the sauce. Serve.

Fish Tacos

There's no need for deep-fried fish when these citrusy Fish Tacos are so fresh. You can even change up the flavors with your current mood. Add a mango salsa for your staycation or a grilled pineapple salsa when dining al fresco. Switch up the guacamole and tomatoes for fresh avocado slices and a pico de gallo.

- **Hands-On Time: 15 minutes**
- **Cook Time: 3 minutes**

Serves 8

Slaw
½ cup grated cabbage
1 large carrot, peeled and grated
1 small jicama, peeled and julienned
Juice of ½ lime
1 tablespoon olive oil
2 dashes hot sauce
¼ cup chopped fresh cilantro
½ teaspoon sea salt

Fish
1 pound cod, cubed
Juice from ½ lime
2 tablespoons fresh orange juice
1 teaspoon garlic salt
1 teaspoon ground cumin
1 tablespoon olive oil
1 cup water

To Serve
½ cup guacamole
½ cup diced tomatoes
8 (6") soft corn tortillas

1 **For Slaw:** Combine slaw ingredients in a medium bowl. Refrigerate covered for 30 minutes up to overnight.

2 **For Fish:** In a large bowl, combine fish, lime juice, orange juice, garlic salt, cumin, and olive oil and refrigerate for 15 minutes.

3 Add 1 cup water to Instant Pot®. Insert trivet. Place steamer basket on top of trivet. Add cod in an even row onto steamer basket. Pour in additional marinade for the steaming aromatics. Lock lid.

4 Press the Manual button and adjust time to 3 minutes. When timer beeps, quick-release pressure until float valve drops and then unlock lid. Transfer fish to a serving bowl.

5 **To Serve:** Assemble fish tacos by adding equal amounts of fish, slaw, guacamole, and tomatoes to each corn tortilla.

Homemade Guacamole

Combine the following ingredients in a medium bowl for a quick-and-easy guacamole: 2 diced avocados, juice from 1 lime, 3 minced garlic cloves, 1 teaspoon hot sauce, 1 diced Roma tomato, 1 teaspoon sea salt, and 2–4 tablespoons chopped cilantro. Refrigerate covered until ready to serve. Should be used within 1–2 days.

Paprika Catfish with Fresh Tarragon

PALEO, GLUTEN-FREE

With the Instant Pot® you can prepare this stewlike dish in no time. It is a great alternative to the traditional catfish fish fry. Not all catfish has to have a Deep-South fry on it. These fresh flavors and the steam cooking give new life to this fish.

- **Hands-On Time: 5 minutes**
- **Cook Time: 3 minutes**

Serves 2

1 (14.5-ounce) can diced tomatoes, including juice
2 teaspoons dried minced onion
¼ teaspoon onion powder
1 teaspoon dried minced garlic
¼ teaspoon garlic powder
2 teaspoons smoked paprika
1 tablespoon chopped fresh tarragon
1 medium green bell pepper, seeded and diced
1 stalk celery, finely diced
1 teaspoon salt
¼ teaspoon ground black pepper
1 pound catfish fillets, rinsed and cut into bite-sized pieces

1 Add all ingredients except fish to the Instant Pot® and stir to mix. Once mixed, add the fish on top. Lock lid.

2 Press the Manual button and adjust time to 3 minutes. When timer beeps, quick-release pressure until float valve drops and then unlock lid.

3 Transfer all ingredients to a serving bowl. Serve warm.

Coconut Curry Sea Bass

PALEO, GLUTEN-FREE

The sturdiness and richness of the sea bass holds up well to the deep flavors of the coconut curry sauce without taking away from the bass's buttery flakiness. If your diet allows it, serve this fish and its sauce over rice or even some steamed spiralized veggie noodles.

- **Hands-On Time: 5 minutes**
- **Cook Time: 3 minutes**

Serves 3

1 (14.5-ounce) can coconut milk
Juice of 1 lime
1 tablespoon red curry paste
1 teaspoon fish sauce
1 teaspoon coconut aminos
1 teaspoon honey
2 teaspoons sriracha
2 cloves garlic, minced
1 teaspoon ground turmeric
1 teaspoon ground ginger
½ teaspoon sea salt
½ teaspoon white pepper
1 pound sea bass, cut into 1" cubes
¼ cup chopped fresh cilantro
3 lime wedges

1 In a large bowl, whisk together coconut milk, lime juice, red curry paste, fish sauce, coconut aminos, honey, sriracha, garlic, turmeric, ginger, sea salt, and white pepper.

2 Place sea bass in the bottom of Instant Pot®. Pour coconut milk mixture over the fish. Lock lid.

3 Press the Manual button and adjust time to 3 minutes. When timer beeps, quick-release pressure until float valve drops and then unlock lid.

4 Transfer fish and broth into three bowls. Garnish each with equal amounts of chopped cilantro and a lime wedge. Serve.

Umami Calamari

You can probably tell if a food is sweet, bitter, sour, or salty when you put it in your mouth. But what about umami? Umami is defined as the "savory" taste, and scientists now recognize it as a distinct taste in addition to the other well-known ones. The anchovy paste in this recipe adds this umami flavor and makes this unexpected calamari dish even more unique.

- **Hands-On Time: 15 minutes**
- **Cook Time: 20 minutes**

Serves 4

1 tablespoon olive oil

1 small onion, peeled and diced

2 cloves garlic, minced

¼ cup dry red wine

1 (14.5-ounce) can diced tomatoes, including juice

1 cup chicken broth

¼ cup chopped fresh parsley

6 tablespoons chopped fresh basil, divided

1 teaspoon sea salt

½ teaspoon ground black pepper

2 teaspoons anchovy paste

1 bay leaf

1 pound calamari tubes, cut into ¼" rings

¼ cup grated Parmesan cheese

1 Press the Sauté button on Instant Pot®. Add olive oil and heat. Add onion and sauté for 3–5 minutes until onions are translucent. Add garlic and sauté for an additional minute. Add red wine, press Adjust button to change temperature to Less, and simmer unlidded for 5 minutes.

2 Add remaining ingredients except 2 tablespoons basil and Parmesan cheese. Lock lid.

3 Press the Manual button and adjust time to 10 minutes. When timer beeps, let pressure release naturally for 10 minutes. Quick-release any additional pressure until the float valve drops and then unlock lid.

4 Remove bay leaf. Use a slotted spoon to transfer pot ingredients to four bowls. Garnish each bowl with equal amounts Parmesan cheese and ½ tablespoon basil.

Fresh or Frozen?

Fresh or frozen, calamari is sold in many forms. Although this recipe calls for slicing calamari tubes, the rings can be found already cut. If you are adventurous, purchase whole squid and break down the entire animal. Just be careful of the ink sac!

Low-Country Boil

You'll notice that the shrimp required in this tasty Instant Pot® recipe are frozen. Shrimp have a much lower cooking time than some of the other Low-Country Boil ingredients, so it helps if your shrimp are frozen so they don't overcook and dry out. If you have fresh shrimp, freeze them for an hour after cleaning before adding them to the dish.

- **Hands-On Time: 10 minutes**
- **Cook Time: 5 minutes**

Serves 6

1 large sweet onion, peeled and chopped
4 cloves garlic, quartered
6 small red potatoes, cut in sixths
3 ears corn, cut in thirds
1½ pounds fully cooked andouille sausage, cut in 1" sections
1 pound frozen tail-on shrimp
1 tablespoon Old Bay Seasoning
2 cups chicken broth
1 lemon, cut into 6 wedges
½ cup chopped fresh parsley

1 Layer onions in an even layer in the Instant Pot®. Scatter the garlic on top of onions. Add red potatoes in an even layer, then do the same for the corn and sausage. Add the shrimp and sprinkle with Old Bay Seasoning. Pour in broth.

2 Squeeze lemon wedges into the Instant Pot® and place squeezed lemon wedges into the Instant Pot®. Lock lid.

3 Press the Manual button and adjust time to 5 minutes. When timer beeps, quick-release the pressure until float valve drops and then unlock lid. Transfer ingredients to a serving platter and garnish with parsley.

Pack a Picnic

This Low-Country Boil is a great summer food. Line a picnic table with newspapers and pour all of the ingredients onto the paper in the middle of the table. Guests can enjoy this family style with no real etiquette to the meal other than to have fun. Oh, and don't forget a roll or two of paper towels. This can get messy.

Mediterranean Cod

PALEO, GLUTEN-FREE

The flavors of the Mediterranean are spotlighted in this simple yet elegant dish. The richness of the olive oil, the freshness of the basil and tomatoes, and the brininess of the kalamata olives all come together to dress up this understated, flaky piece of cod.

- **Hands-On Time: 5 minutes**
- **Cook Time: 6 minutes**

Serves 2

2 (5-ounce) cod fillets, divided

2 teaspoons olive oil, divided

1½ teaspoons sea salt, divided

10 pitted kalamata olives, divided

1 small Roma tomato, diced, divided

3 tablespoons chopped fresh basil leaves, divided

1 Place a piece of cod on a 10" × 10" square of aluminum foil. Drizzle with 1 teaspoon olive oil. Sprinkle with ½ teaspoon salt. Scatter 5 olives, ½ the tomatoes, and 1 tablespoon basil on top of fish. Bring up the sides of the foil and crimp at the top to create a foil pocket.

2 Repeat with remaining piece of fish. Place both fish packs in the Instant Pot®. Lock lid.

3 Press the Manual button and adjust time to 6 minutes. When the timer beeps, quick-release pressure until float valve drops and then unlock lid.

4 Remove foil packets and transfer fish and toppings to two plates. Garnish each plate with ½ tablespoon basil and ¼ teaspoon salt.

Dilly Lemon Salmon

PALEO, GLUTEN-FREE

Known for its beneficial omega-3 fatty acids, salmon is also high in vitamin B_{12}, vitamin D, and selenium, among others. Do your body good and quickly steam this very mild and flaky fish in the Instant Pot®.

- **Hands-On Time: 5 minutes**
- **Cook Time: 5 minutes**

Serves 2

2 (5-ounce) salmon fillets
½ teaspoon sea salt
4 lemon slices
2 teaspoons chopped fresh
   dill
1 cup water

1 Pat fillets dry with a paper towel and place on a steamer basket. Season salmon with salt. Place 2 lemon slices on each fillet. Sprinkle with chopped dill.

2 Place water in Instant Pot®. Insert trivet. Place steamer basket onto trivet. Lock lid.

3 Press the Manual button and adjust time to 5 minutes. When timer beeps, quick-release the pressure until float valve drops and then unlock lid.

4 Remove fish to plates and serve immediately.

Lobster Risotto

GLUTEN-FREE

Step up the richness of this dish by making a quick lobster broth that you can sub in for the vegetable broth used in the recipe. In a medium saucepan over high heat, add 3 cups of vegetable broth and the shells from the lobster. Bring to a boil. Reduce heat. Cover and let simmer for 20 minutes. Remove the saucepan from the heat and set aside to cool. Strain out lobster shells and you have just created a quick and easy lobster broth. But no matter which broth you use, if your risotto is too thick, add a little more broth, 1 tablespoon at a time, until you're happy with the consistency. Then all you have to do is sit back and enjoy!

- **Hands-On Time: 5 minutes**
- **Cook Time: 20 minutes**

Serves 4

4 tablespoons butter

1 small onion, peeled and finely diced

2 cloves garlic, minced

1½ cups Arborio rice

1 cup chardonnay

3 cups vegetable broth

½ teaspoon lemon zest

3 tablespoons grated Parmesan cheese

½ teaspoon salt

¼ teaspoon ground black pepper

Meat from 3 small lobster tails, diced

¼ cup chopped fresh parsley

1 Press the Sauté button on the Instant Pot® and add the butter. Heat until melted. Add onion and stir-fry for 3–5 minutes until translucent. Add garlic and rice and cook for an additional minute. Add white wine and slowly stir unlidded for 5 minutes until liquid is absorbed by the rice.

2 Add broth, lemon zest, Parmesan, salt, and pepper. Lock lid.

3 Press the Rice button (the Instant Pot® will determine the cook time; 1½ cups rice takes about 10 minutes pressurized cooking time). Let pressure release naturally for 10 minutes. Quick-release any additional pressure until float valve drops and then unlock lid.

4 Stir in lobster, garnish with fresh parsley, and serve warm.

Mahi-Mahi with a Lemon-Caper Butter Sauce

GLUTEN-FREE

Mahi-mahi is a firm fish that works well as a vessel for whatever flavors you cook it with. It is mild in taste and doesn't have that "fishy" flavor that you get when you use tuna or salmon.

- **Hands-On Time: 5 minutes**
- **Cook Time: 7 minutes**

Serves 2

2 (6-ounce, 1"-thick) mahi-mahi fillets

2 tablespoons fresh lemon juice

2 tablespoons capers

1 teaspoon sea salt

1 teaspoon lemon zest

2 tablespoons butter, cut into 2 pats

1 tablespoon chopped fresh parsley

1 Place a piece of foil on the Instant Pot®'s steamer basket. Set both fillets on the foil. Create a "boat" with the foil by bringing up the edges. Pour lemon juice on fish. Add capers. Season fish with salt and zest. Add a pat of butter to each fillet. Set trivet in the Instant Pot® and place the steamer basket on the trivet. Lock lid.

2 Press the Manual button and adjust time to 7 minutes. Quick-release pressure until float valve drops and then unlock lid.

3 Transfer fish to two plates. Garnish each with ½ tablespoon chopped parsley.

Steamed Shrimp and Asparagus

In a busy world and a busy kitchen, this dish of shrimp and asparagus is simplicity at its best. With few ingredients, but a distinctly delicious taste, this straightforward and uncomplicated recipe is perfect for those times when the world seems just a little too busy.

- **Hands-On Time: 5 minutes**
- **Cook Time: 1 minute**

Serves 2

1 cup water
1 bunch asparagus
1 teaspoon sea salt, divided
1 pound shrimp, peeled and
    deveined
½ lemon
2 tablespoons butter, cut
    into 2 pats

1 Pour water into Instant Pot®. Insert trivet. Place steamer basket onto trivet.

2 Prepare asparagus by finding the natural snap point on the stalks and discarding the woody ends.

3 Spread the asparagus on the bottom of the steamer basket. Sprinkle with ½ teaspoon salt. Add the shrimp. Squeeze lemon into the Instant Pot®, then sprinkle shrimp with remaining ½ teaspoon salt. Place pats of butter on shrimp. Lock lid.

4 Press the Manual button and adjust time to 1 minute. When the timer beeps, quick-release the pressure until the float valve drops and then unlock lid.

5 Transfer shrimp and asparagus to a platter and serve.

Steamed Crab Legs

PALEO, GLUTEN-FREE

These crab legs are great served with melted butter, especially clarified butter, or ghee. Serve with plenty of lemon wedges. The wedges are not only great squeezed over the freshly cracked crabmeat, but they act as a great hand cleaner and odor remover once you are done with this very interactive meal.

- **Hands-On Time: 5 minutes**
- **Cook Time: 3 minutes**

Serves 2

1 cup water
4 cloves garlic, quartered
1 small onion, peeled and diced large
1 tablespoon Old Bay Seasoning
2 sprigs fresh thyme
2 pounds crab legs

1 Add water, garlic, onion, Old Bay Seasoning, and thyme to the Instant Pot®; stir to combine.

2 Insert trivet. Add crab legs. Lock lid.

3 Press the Steam button and adjust time to 3 minutes. When the timer beeps, quick-release the pressure until float valve drops and then unlock lid.

4 Transfer crab legs to a serving platter.

Louisiana Grouper

PALEO, GLUTEN-FREE

Creole seasoning is a somewhat vague ingredient on this recipe list. Look in your local grocer's spice aisle and there will be several versions. Choose the one that speaks to you as you just can't go wrong with these beautiful spice blends.

- **Hands-On Time: 10 minutes**
- **Cook Time: 20 minutes**

Serves 4

2 tablespoons olive oil

1 small onion, peeled and diced

1 stalk celery, diced

1 small green bell pepper, seeded and diced

1 (15-ounce) can diced tomatoes

¼ cup water

1 tablespoon tomato paste

1 teaspoon honey

Pinch of dried basil

2 teaspoons Creole seasoning

4 grouper fillets, rinsed and cut into bite-sized pieces

½ teaspoon sea salt

¼ teaspoon ground black pepper

1 Press Sauté button on Instant Pot®. Heat oil and add onion, celery, and bell pepper. Sauté for 3–5 minutes until onions are translucent and peppers are tender.

2 Stir in undrained tomatoes, water, tomato paste, honey, basil, and Creole seasoning.

3 Sprinkle fish with salt and pepper. Gently toss the fish pieces into the sauce in the Instant Pot®. Lock lid.

4 Press the Manual button and adjust time to 5 minutes. When timer beeps, quick-release the pressure until float valve drops and then unlock lid.

5 Transfer fish to a serving platter. Press Sauté button on Instant Pot®, press Adjust button to change the temperature to Less, and simmer juices unlidded for 10 minutes. Transfer tomatoes and preferred amount of sauce over fish. Serve immediately.

Steamed Mussels in White Wine

PALEO, GLUTEN-FREE

Fairly inexpensive, mussels are a great seafood to put in your family's rotation of meals. These bivalve buddies are sweet and tasty. To dress up this dish, serve over linguini and add some crusty bread on the side.

- **Hands-On Time: 10 minutes**
- **Cook Time: 8 minutes**

Serves 4

2 tablespoons ghee

1 medium onion, peeled and diced

3 cloves garlic, minced

½ cup dry white wine

1 (14.5-ounce) can diced tomatoes, including juice

1 teaspoon cayenne pepper

1 teaspoon sea salt

Juice of 1 lemon

2 pounds fresh mussels, cleaned and debearded

4 tablespoons chopped fresh parsley

1 Press the Sauté button on Instant Pot®. Add the ghee and melt. Add onion and sauté for 3–5 minutes until translucent. Add garlic and cook for an additional minute. Stir in white wine and let cook 2 minutes. Add tomatoes, cayenne pepper, salt, and lemon juice.

2 Insert steamer basket. Place mussels on top. Lock lid.

3 Press the Manual button and adjust time to 0 minutes. When timer beeps, quick-release pressure until float valve drops and then unlock lid.

4 Remove mussels and discard any that haven't opened. Transfer mussels to four bowls and pour liquid from Instant Pot® equally among bowls. Garnish each bowl with 1 tablespoon parsley. Serve immediately.

Creamed Crab

Although this recipe is insanely good by the spoonful on its own, use this to level-up some simple dishes. Serve this crab atop a cod fillet with some fresh asparagus or even next to a grilled steak for a little surf and turf.

- **Hands-On Time: 5 minutes**
- **Cook Time: 8 minutes**

Serves 4

4 tablespoons butter

½ stalk celery, finely diced

1 small red onion, peeled and finely diced

1 pound uncooked lump crabmeat

¼ cup chicken broth

½ cup heavy cream

½ teaspoon sea salt

½ teaspoon ground black pepper

1   Press the Sauté button on Instant Pot®. Add the butter and melt. Add the celery and red onion. Stir-fry for 3–5 minutes until celery begins to soften. Stir in the crabmeat and broth. Lock lid.

2   Press the Manual button and adjust time to 3 minutes. Press the Pressure button to change the pressure to Less. When timer beeps, quick-release pressure until float valve drops and then unlock lid.

3   Carefully stir in the cream, add salt and pepper, and serve warm.

Choosing Crab

Fresh, lump crabmeat is the best option for this recipe—but it can be pricey. Fortunately, there are many different varieties and sections of the crab that can be purchased at a lower price point. It is even sold in cans like the more familiar tuna. Although there is imitation crab available, draw the line with this. It is stringy and packed with starch and chemicals.

Steamed Clams

Serve these clams atop a pile of linguini with a piece of crusty bread on the side. To make this option even more special, substitute a can of diced tomatoes, including juice, for the water to create a warm, hearty linguini sauce.

- **Hands-On Time: 5 minutes**
- **Cook Time: 10 minutes**

Serves 4

2 pounds fresh clams, rinsed and purged

1 tablespoon olive oil

1 small white onion, peeled and diced

1 clove garlic, quartered

½ cup chardonnay

½ cup water

1 Place clams in the steamer basket. Set aside.

2 Press the Sauté button on Instant Pot®. Heat olive oil. Add onion and sauté 3–5 minutes until translucent. Add garlic and cook another minute. Pour in white wine and water. Insert steamer basket. Lock lid.

3 Press the Manual button and adjust time to 4 minutes. When the timer beeps, quick-release pressure until lid unlocks.

4 Transfer clams to four serving bowls and top with a generous scoop of cooking liquid.

How Do You Purge Clams?

Soak your clams in water with 1–2 tablespoons of cornmeal for 20 minutes. Rinse and drain until there is no more sand.

Vegetarian Main Dishes

Isn't the Instant Pot® just for tenderizing meats? Not quite. The Instant Pot® is a multifunctional kitchen gadget that is incredible at cooking beans and rice and steaming vegetables. No longer will you have to soak beans for hours on end. You can now take those little hard pebbles and have beautifully spiced and tender beans within 30 minutes. In addition, rice, millet, bulgur, couscous, and all of the other grains in those bulk bins that you have wanted to experiment with are cooked to perfection in an Instant Pot®. The pressure and the steam create some deliciously moist and tender meals.

And don't forget about those glorious veggies because they can be steamed perfectly in minutes retaining nutrients and ensuring tenderness by pressure cooking. From Zucchini Pomodoro to Taco Salad to Mushroom Risotto, this chapter has much to offer in flavor and variety where a lot of vegetarian meals traditionally fall short.

White Bean Cassoulet

This hearty recipe was traditionally cooked in a dish called a *cassole*, originating in the south of France and generally slow-cooked with a meat of some sort. This Instant Pot® dish is made with beans and vegetables and is great served with some crusty artisanal bread to sop up all of the goodness.

- **Hands-On Time: 5 minutes**
- **Cook Time: 45 minutes**

Serves 6

1 tablespoon olive oil

1 medium onion, peeled and diced

2 cups dried cannellini beans

1 medium parsnip, peeled and diced small

2 medium carrots, peeled and diced small

2 stalks celery, diced

1 medium zucchini, diced large

½ teaspoon fennel seed

¼ teaspoon ground nutmeg

½ teaspoon garlic powder

1 teaspoon sea salt

½ teaspoon ground black pepper

2 cups vegetable broth

1 (14.5-ounce) can diced tomatoes, including juice

2 sprigs rosemary

1 Press the Sauté button on Instant Pot®. Heat oil Add onion and stir-fry 3–5 minutes until onions are translucent. Add beans and toss.

2 Add a layer of diced parsnips, then a layer of carrots, and next a layer of celery. Finally, add a layer of zucchini. Sprinkle in fennel seed, nutmeg, garlic powder, salt, and pepper.

3 Gently pour in broth and canned tomatoes. Then add rosemary. Lock lid.

4 Press the Bean button and cook for the default time of 30 minutes. When timer beeps, let pressure release naturally for 10 minutes. Quick-release any additional pressure until float valve drops and then unlock lid.

5 Press the Sauté button on the Instant Pot®, press the Adjust button to change the temperature to Less, and simmer bean mixture unlidded for 10 minutes to thicken. Transfer to a serving bowl and carefully toss. Discard rosemary and serve.

Zucchini Pomodoro

PALEO, GLUTEN-FREE

This recipe calls for spiralized zucchini, but if you don't have a vegetable spiralizer, you can manually cut the zucchini into long strips. However, the spiralizer is a great, inexpensive kitchen gadget that gives you a lot of bang for the buck. It can spiral apples, jicama, and carrots for summer salads as well as any root vegetable you'd like to substitute for pasta.

- **Hands-On Time: 10 minutes**
- **Cook Time: 12 minutes**

Serves 4

1 tablespoon avocado oil

1 large onion, peeled and diced

3 cloves garlic, minced

1 (28-ounce) can diced tomatoes, including juice

½ cup water

1 tablespoon Italian seasoning

1 teaspoon sea salt

½ teaspoon ground black pepper

2 medium zucchini, spiraled

1 Press Sauté button on the Instant Pot®. Heat avocado oil. Add onions and stir-fry for 3–5 minutes until translucent. Add garlic and cook for an additional minute. Add tomatoes, water, Italian seasoning, salt, and pepper. Add zucchini and toss to combine. Lock lid.

2 Press the Manual button and adjust time to 1 minute. When timer beeps, let pressure release naturally for 5 minutes. Quick-release any additional pressure until float valve drops and then unlock lid.

3 Transfer zucchini to four bowls. Press Sauté button, press Adjust button to change the temperature to Less, and simmer sauce in the Instant Pot® unlidded for 5 minutes. Ladle over zucchini and serve immediately.

Asian Mushroom Sweet Potato Noodles

PALEO, GLUTEN-FREE

The Asian flavors found in this dish are a perfect match for these oodles of sweet potato noodles that are easily steamed in the Instant Pot®. The shiitake mushrooms add a meatiness to this dish—along with their health-promoting qualities and immune-boosting benefits.

- **Hands-On Time: 5 minutes**
- **Cook Time: 3 minutes**

Serves 4

2 tablespoons coconut aminos
1 tablespoon white vinegar
2 teaspoons olive oil
1 teaspoon sesame oil
1 tablespoon honey
¼ teaspoon red pepper flakes
3 cloves garlic, minced
1 large sweet potato, peeled and spiraled
1 pound shiitake mushrooms, sliced
1 cup vegetable broth
¼ cup chopped fresh parsley

1. In a large bowl, whisk together coconut aminos, vinegar, olive oil, sesame oil, honey, red pepper flakes, and garlic.

2. Toss sweet potato and shiitake mushrooms in sauce. Refrigerate covered for 30 minutes.

3. Pour vegetable broth into Instant Pot®. Add trivet. Lower steamer basket onto trivet and add the sweet potato mixture to the basket. Lock lid.

4. Press the Manual button and adjust time to 3 minutes. When timer beeps, let pressure release naturally for 5 minutes. Quick-release any additional pressure until float valve drops and then unlock lid.

5. Remove basket from the Instant Pot® and distribute sweet potatoes and mushrooms evenly among four bowls; pour liquid from the Instant Pot® over bowls and garnish with chopped parsley.

Taco Salad

You don't need beef or chicken to enjoy a hearty taco salad. In this vegetarian dish, perfectly seasoned beans are served atop mixed greens with fresh toppings. Welcome to Taco Tuesday!

- **Hands-On Time: 10 minutes**
- **Cook Time: 45 minutes**

Serves 6

½ cup dried black beans
½ cup dried red beans
1 tablespoon avocado oil
1 small onion, peeled and diced
2 cups vegetable broth
½ teaspoon garlic powder
½ teaspoon chili powder
½ teaspoon ground cumin
½ teaspoon sea salt
¼ cup chopped fresh cilantro
6 cups mixed greens
1 medium avocado, pitted and sliced
2 large tomatoes, diced
1 cup corn kernels
½ cup sour cream
24 tortilla chips

1. Rinse and drain beans.

2. Press the Sauté button on Instant Pot®. Heat oil. Add onion and stir-fry 3–5 minutes until onions are translucent. Deglaze the Instant Pot® by adding broth and scraping the bottom and sides of the Instant Pot®.

3. Add beans, garlic powder, chili powder, cumin, salt, and cilantro. Lock lid.

4. Press the Bean button and cook for the default time of 30 minutes. When the timer beeps, let pressure release naturally for 10 minutes. Quick-release any additional pressure until float valve drops and then unlock lid.

5. Press Sauté button, press Adjust button to change the temperature to Less, and simmer bean mixture unlidded for 10 minutes to thicken.

6. Distribute mixed greens evenly among six bowls. Add a spoonful of beans to each bowl. Garnish with equal amounts of avocado, tomatoes, corn, and sour cream. Top each with 4 tortilla chips and serve.

Millet Eggplant Pilaf

This twist on a traditional rice pilaf side dish is hearty enough to serve as a complete meal. Among other properties, millet provides protein and is a good source of magnesium. The eggplant provides a great source of fiber and adds a meatiness to the dish. In addition, the flavors are brought together in just minutes.

- **Hands-On Time: 5 minutes**
- **Cook Time: 17 minutes**

Serves 4

1 tablespoon butter
¼ cup peeled and diced onion
1 cup peeled and diced eggplant
1 small Roma tomato, seeded and diced
1 cup millet
2 cups vegetable broth
1 teaspoon sea salt
¼ teaspoon ground black pepper
⅛ teaspoon saffron
⅛ teaspoon cayenne pepper
1 tablespoon chopped fresh chives

1 Press Sauté button on Instant Pot®. Add butter and melt. Add onion and cook 3–5 minutes until translucent. Toss in eggplant and stir-fry for 2 more minutes. Add diced tomato.

2 Add millet to Instant Pot® in an even layer. Gently pour in broth. Lock lid.

3 Press the Rice button (the Instant Pot® will determine the time, about 10 minutes pressurized cooking time). When timer beeps, let pressure release naturally for 5 minutes. Quick-release any additional pressure until float valve drops and then unlock lid.

4 Transfer pot ingredients to a serving bowl. Season with salt, pepper, saffron, and cayenne pepper. Garnish with chives.

Saucy Millet and Corn

This easy recipe is not only quick, but you probably have most of the ingredients in your pantry. The Gruyère adds a little bite and nuttiness to this recipe; however, feel free to substitute the similar-tasting Swiss cheese or even add grated Parmesan cheese to give it a different flavor profile.

- **Hands-On Time: 5 minutes**
- **Cook Time: 10 minutes**

Serves 4

2 teaspoons olive oil
1 cup millet
2 cups vegetable broth
1 teaspoon sea salt
1 (15.25-ounce) can corn kernels
1 (8-ounce) can tomato sauce
¼ cup grated Gruyère cheese

1 Drizzle 2 teaspoons olive oil in Instant Pot®. Layer millet into pot. Add vegetable broth and salt. Lock lid.

2 Press the Rice button (the Instant Pot® will determine the cooking time, about 10 minutes pressurized cooking time). When timer beeps, let pressure release naturally for 5 minutes. Quick-release any additional pressure until float valve drops and then unlock lid.

3 Transfer millet to a serving bowl. Toss corn, tomato sauce, and Gruyère cheese in millet. Serve warm.

Mushroom Risotto

The meatiness and heartiness of the mushrooms in this dish balance perfectly with the creaminess and decadence of the risotto. To change up this dish, play around with some of the wild mushrooms available or even consider using a combination of them.

- **Hands-On Time: 5 minutes**
- **Cook Time: 20 minutes**

Serves 4

4 tablespoons butter

1 small onion, peeled and finely diced

4 cups sliced baby bella mushrooms

2 cloves garlic, minced

1½ cups Arborio rice

4 cups vegetable broth, divided

3 tablespoons grated Parmesan cheese

½ teaspoon salt

¼ teaspoon ground black pepper

2 tablespoons fresh thyme leaves

1 Press the Sauté button on the Instant Pot®. Add the butter and melt. Add the onion and stir-fry for 3–5 minutes until onions are translucent. Add mushrooms, garlic, and rice and cook for an additional minute. Add 1 cup broth and stir unlidded until liquid is absorbed by the rice.

2 Add remaining 3 cups broth, Parmesan cheese, salt, and pepper. Lock lid.

3 Press the Rice button (the Instant Pot® will determine the cooking time; 1½ cups rice takes about 10 minutes pressurized cooking time). Let pressure release naturally for 10 minutes. Quick-release any additional pressure until float valve drops and then unlock lid.

4 Transfer to a serving bowl and garnish with thyme and serve.

Wheat Berry Salad

Chewier in texture and nuttier in flavor than most grains, wheat berries are a nutritional mother lode. Consisting of the bran, germ, and endosperm of the wheat kernel, wheat berries contain protein, fiber, and B_6 vitamins, making it a grain powerhouse. This zippy salad is excellent as a standalone meal or served as a side dish. Also, feel free to garnish with snipped chives to take this dish up a notch and impress your guests.

- **Hands-On Time: 5 minutes**
- **Cook Time: 35 minutes**

6 servings

3 tablespoons olive oil, divided

1 cup wheat berries

2¼ cups water, divided

2 cups peeled and shredded carrots

2 apples, peeled, cored, and diced small

½ cup raisins

2 tablespoons pure maple syrup

2 teaspoons orange zest

¼ cup fresh orange juice

1 tablespoon balsamic vinegar

½ teaspoon salt

1 Press Sauté button on Instant Pot®. Heat 1 tablespoon oil and add wheat berries. Stir-fry for 4–5 minutes until browned and fragrant. Add 2 cups water. Lock lid.

2 Press the Manual button and adjust time to 30 minutes. When timer beeps, let pressure release naturally for 10 minutes. Quick-release any additional pressure until float valve drops and then unlock lid.

3 Let cool for 10 minutes and drain any additional liquid.

4 Transfer cooled berries to a medium bowl and add remaining ingredients. Refrigerate covered overnight until ready to serve chilled.

Stuffed Bell Peppers

Loaded with veggies, beans, and rice, these peppers are cooked to tender perfection in the Instant Pot®. Use this recipe as a substantial side dish or even as a meal on its own.

- **Hands-On Time: 15 minutes**
- **Cook Time: 15 minutes**

Serves 4

4 large bell peppers
2 cups cooked white rice
1 medium onion, peeled and diced
3 small Roma tomatoes, diced
¼ cup marinara sauce
1 cup corn kernels (cut from the cob is preferred)
¼ cup sliced black olives
¼ cup canned cannellini beans, rinsed and drained
¼ cup canned black beans, rinsed and drained
1 teaspoon sea salt
1 teaspoon garlic powder
½ cup vegetable broth
2 tablespoons grated Parmesan cheese

1. Cut off the bell pepper tops as close to the tops as possible. Hollow out and discard seeds. Poke a few small holes in the bottom of the peppers to allow drippings to drain.

2. In a medium bowl, combine remaining ingredients except for broth and Parmesan cheese. Stuff equal amounts of mixture into each of the bell peppers.

3. Place trivet into the Instant Pot® and pour in the broth. Set the peppers upright on the trivet. Lock lid.

4. Press the Manual button and adjust time to 15 minutes. When timer beeps, let pressure release naturally until float valve drops and then unlock lid.

5. Serve immediately and garnish with Parmesan cheese.

Macaroni and Cheese

Thanks to the Instant Pot® this is the easiest mac-n-cheese that you'll ever make. You need less than ten minutes to create a creamy, delicious, vegetarian meal that your family will ask for again and again. And if you like a creamier sauce, add more milk, 1 tablespoon at a time, until it's perfect!

- **Hands-On Time: 5 minutes**
- **Cook Time: 4 minutes**

Serves 6

1 pound elbow macaroni
¼ cup milk
1 cup shredded sharp Cheddar
¼ cup ricotta cheese
2 tablespoons grated Parmesan cheese
2 tablespoons butter
½ teaspoon ground mustard
2 teaspoons salt
½ teaspoon ground black pepper

1 Place macaroni in an even layer in Instant Pot®. Pour enough water to come about ¼" over pasta. Lock lid.

2 Press the Manual button and adjust time to 4 minutes. When the timer beeps, let the pressure release naturally for 3 minutes. Quick-release any additional pressure until float valve drops and then unlock lid.

3 Drain any residual water. Add milk, Cheddar, ricotta, Parmesan, butter, mustard, salt, and pepper. Stir in the warmed pot until well-combined. Serve warm.

Bowtie Pasta with Pesto

Although homemade pesto is very easy to make, there are many bottled versions sold that are amazing. You can use anything from traditional basil pesto to artichoke pesto, sun-dried tomato pesto, and mint pesto in this dish. There are many from which to choose, so make this dish more than once and try them all.

- **Hands-On Time: 2 minutes**
- **Cook Time: 4 minutes**

Serves 6

1 pound bowtie pasta
¾ cup pesto
¼ cup grated Parmesan
   cheese

1 Place macaroni in an even layer in Instant Pot®. Pour enough water to come about ¼" over pasta. Lock lid.

2 Press the Manual button and adjust time to 4 minutes. When the timer beeps, let the pressure release naturally for 3 minutes. Quick-release any additional pressure until float valve drops and lid unlocks.

3 Drain any residual water except for 2 tablespoons; transfer pasta and reserved cooking water to a serving bowl. Combine with pesto. Garnish with Parmesan cheese and serve.

Penne with Mushroom-Tomato Sauce

This flavorful penne dish will become a staple in your home. Although the ingredients are simple and inexpensive, the marriage of flavors in this economical meal come together and fly your imagination straight to Rome. Right before serving, drizzle just a touch of olive oil over each serving for an extra touch of Italy.

- **Hands-On Time: 10 minutes**
- **Cook Time: 10 minutes**

Serves 6

1 tablespoon olive oil

1 medium onion, peeled and diced

2 cups sliced mushrooms

1 large zucchini, diced

1 (2.25-ounce) can sliced black olives

1 (45-ounce) jar pasta sauce

1 pound penne pasta

½ cup vegetable broth

½ cup chopped fresh basil leaves

1 Press the Sauté button on Instant Pot®. Heat olive oil. Add onion and mushrooms and cook for 3–5 minutes until onions are translucent. Add zucchini. Toss in olives, pasta sauce, and pasta. Add broth. Lock lid.

2 Press the Manual button and adjust time to 4 minutes. When the timer beeps, let the pressure release naturally for 3 minutes. Quick-release any additional pressure until float valve drops and then unlock lid.

3 Garnish with basil leaves and serve.

Seasoned Black Beans

This simple dish packs a punch of south-of-the-border flavor. Serve this dish as a side or add to your favorite taco recipe to get rid of the ho-hum of your regular recipe.

- **Hands-On Time: 5 minutes**
- **Cook Time: 45 minutes**

Serves 8

1 cup dried black beans
1 tablespoon olive oil
1 small onion, peeled and diced
3 cloves garlic, minced
2 cups vegetable broth
¼ teaspoon ground coriander
½ teaspoon chili powder
¼ teaspoon ground cumin
½ teaspoon sea salt
2 teaspoons Italian seasoning

1 Rinse and drain beans.

2 Press the Sauté button on Instant Pot®. Heat olive oil and add onion. Stir-fry 3–5 minutes until onions are translucent. Add garlic and sauté for an additional minute. Deglaze the Instant Pot® by adding broth and scraping the bottom and sides of Instant Pot®.

3 Add beans and remaining ingredients. Lock lid.

4 Press the Bean button and cook for the default time of 30 minutes. When timer beeps, let pressure release naturally for 10 minutes. Quick-release any additional pressure until float valve drops and then unlock lid.

5 Press Sauté button, press Adjust button to change the temperature to Less, and simmer bean mixture unlidded for 10 minutes to thicken.

6 With a slotted spoon, transfer beans to a serving bowl.

Quinoa Endive Boats

With endive, nature has created a little boat ready for you to fill. The simplicity of the seasoned quinoa stuffing and the crunchiness and nuttiness of the roasted pecan garnish temper the somewhat bitterness of the endive to make a well-rounded bite.

- **Hands-On Time: 10 minutes**
- **Cook Time: 3 minutes**

Serves 4

1 tablespoon walnut oil

1 cup quinoa

2½ cups water

2 cups chopped jarred artichoke hearts

2 cups diced tomatoes, seeded

½ small red onion, peeled and thinly sliced

2 tablespoons olive oil

1 tablespoon balsamic vinegar

2 heads Belgian endive

1 cup roasted pecans

1 Press the Sauté button on Instant Pot®. Heat walnut oil. Add quinoa and toss for 1 minute until slightly browned. Add water. Lock lid.

2 Press the Manual button and adjust time to 2 minutes. When timer beeps, let pressure release naturally for 10 minutes. Quick-release any additional pressure until float valve drops and then unlock lid. Drain liquid and transfer quinoa to a serving bowl.

3 Toss remaining ingredients except endive leaves and pecans into quinoa. Refrigerate mixture covered until cooled for 1 hour up to overnight.

4 To prepare boats, separate the endive leaves. Rinse, drain, and divide them among four plates. Top each with ¼ of the quinoa mixture. Distribute ¼ cup toasted pecans over the top of each endive boat and serve.

Turnip and Carrot Purée

This flavorful mash of root vegetables is a perfect accompaniment to roasted meats and even the Mighty "Meat"loaf (see recipe in this chapter). Enjoy this in a spoon or on a pita crisp as an appetizer.

- **Hands-On Time: 10 minutes**
- **Cook Time: 10 minutes**

Serves 6

2 tablespoons olive oil, divided

3 large turnips, peeled and quartered

4 large carrots, peeled and cut into 2" pieces

2 cups vegetable broth

1 teaspoon salt

½ teaspoon ground nutmeg

2 tablespoons sour cream

1 Press the Sauté button on Instant Pot®. Heat 1 tablespoon olive oil. Toss turnips and carrots in oil for 1 minute. Add broth. Lock lid.

2 Press the Manual button and adjust time to 8 minutes. When timer beeps, quick-release pressure until float valve drops and then unlock lid.

3 Drain vegetables and reserve liquid; set liquid aside. Add 2 tablespoons of reserved liquid plus remaining ingredients to vegetables in the Instant Pot®. Use an immersion blender to blend until desired smoothness. If too thick, add more liquid 1 tablespoon at a time. Serve warm.

Bavarian Kale and Potatoes

If you like German cooking, then this is your side dish. Potatoes are a staple in Germany and each region has a special way of preparing this simple tuber. The potatoes in this recipe are so tenderly cooked in the Instant Pot® that you'd think they had been slow cooking all day. The caraway seeds will give you that familiar flavor found in sauerkraut. This dish is perfect to serve at Oktoberfest with your favorite sausages and pilsner beer!

- **Hands-On Time: 10 minutes**
- **Cook Time: 10 minutes**

Serves 4

1 tablespoon olive oil

1 small onion, peeled and diced

1 stalk celery, diced

2 cloves garlic, minced

4 medium potatoes, peeled and diced

2 bunches kale, washed, deveined, and chopped

1½ cups vegetable broth

2 teaspoons salt

½ teaspoon ground black pepper

¼ teaspoon caraway seeds

1 tablespoon apple cider vinegar

4 tablespoons sour cream

1 Press the Sauté button on Instant Pot®. Heat oil. Add onion and celery and stir-fry 3–5 minutes until onions are translucent. Add garlic and cook for an additional minute. Add potatoes in an even layer. Add chopped kale in an even layer. Add broth. Lock lid.

2 Press the Manual button and adjust time to 5 minutes. Let the pressure release naturally for 10 minutes. Quick-release any additional pressure until float valve drops and then unlock lid; then drain broth.

3 Stir in salt, pepper, caraway seeds, and vinegar; slightly mash the potatoes in the Instant Pot®. Garnish each serving with 1 tablespoon sour cream.

Mighty "Meat"loaf

Who needs beef or pork when this "meat"loaf hits the spot every time? With the meatiness from the mushrooms, the protein from the beans, and the nutrients in the vegetables, this meal delivers on all fronts.

- **Hands-On Time: 15 minutes**
- **Cook Time: 12 minutes**

Serves 4

1 (15-ounce) can cannellini beans, drained and rinsed

1 cup finely chopped baby bella mushrooms

2 small shallots, minced

1 large carrot, peeled and grated

2 garlic cloves, minced

2 large eggs, whisked

1 cup shredded mozzarella cheese

1 tablespoon Italian seasoning

1 teaspoon sea salt

½ teaspoon ground black pepper

1 cup old-fashioned oats

1 tablespoon Dijon mustard

1 (8-ounce) can tomato sauce

1 cup water

1 Add beans to a medium mixing bowl. Using the back of a wooden spoon, smash the beans against the side of the bowl until they all pop open. Add remaining ingredients except water and mix well. Form mixture into a ball and place into a greased 7-cup glass bowl. Slightly press down the top of the ball.

2 Pour 1 cup water into Instant Pot®. Insert trivet. Place glass bowl onto trivet. Lock lid.

3 Press the Manual button and adjust time to 12 minutes. When timer beeps, quick-release pressure until float valve drops and then unlock lid. Remove bowl from Instant Pot® and let cool for 15 minutes before serving.

11

Desserts

If you're like most people, you probably have a sweet tooth that pulls at your stomach from time to time. The great thing about the Instant Pot® is that it creates desserts that are just the right size to make your sweet tooth *and* your scale happy. Most of these desserts provide only 4–6 servings, so you won't be tempted to overeat and you won't have desserts hanging around your kitchen for days on end. And with dishes ranging from Spiced Red Wine–Poached Pears and Carrot Coconut Cake to Steamed Bread Pudding and Creamy Key Lime Pie, these perfect little delights are guaranteed to hit the spot . . . no matter what you find yourself craving.

Stuffed "Baked" Apples

You can have your apples and stuff them, too! After a day of apple picking with the family, this glorious traditional recipe can be cooked and on your plates within 15 minutes. Serve with a scoop of vanilla or cinnamon ice cream to take it over the top!

- **Hands-On Time: 10 minutes**
- **Cook Time: 5 minutes**

Serves 4

½ cup fresh orange juice
½ teaspoon orange zest
¼ cup packed light brown sugar
¼ cup golden raisins
¼ cup chopped pecans
¼ cup quick-cooking oats
½ teaspoon ground cinnamon
4 cooking apples
4 tablespoons butter, divided
1 cup water

1 In a small bowl, mix together orange juice, orange zest, brown sugar, raisins, pecans, oats, and cinnamon. Set aside.

2 Rinse and dry the apples. Cut off the top fourth of each apple. Peel the cut portion of the apple. Dice it and then stir into the oat mixture. Hollow out and core the apples by cutting to, but not through, the apple bottoms.

3 Place each apple on a piece of aluminum foil that is large enough to wrap the apple completely. Fill the apple centers with the oat mixture. Top each with 1 tablespoon butter. Wrap the foil around each apple, folding the foil over at the top and then pinching it firmly together.

4 Pour the water into Instant Pot®. Set in trivet. Place the apple packets on the rack. Lock lid.

5 Press the Manual button and adjust time to 5 minutes. When timer beeps, let pressure release naturally for 10 minutes. Quick-release any additional pressure until float valve drops and then unlock lid.

6 Carefully unwrap apples and transfer to serving plates.

Lemon Cheesecake

If you're looking for a light, summery dessert that's custom-made for a warm day, then you're in luck. This Lemon Cheesecake fits the bill perfectly. Keep things seasonal by topping this popular dessert with fresh berries—strawberries, blueberries, raspberries, or whatever you find for sale at your local farmstand.

- **Hands-On Time: 10 minutes**
- **Cook Time: 30 minutes**

Serves 6

Crust
20 vanilla wafers
1½ tablespoons almond slices, toasted
3 tablespoons melted butter

Cheesecake Filling
12 ounces cream cheese, cubed and room temperature
2 tablespoons sour cream, room temperature
½ cup sugar
2 large eggs, room temperature
Zest of 2 lemons, grated
1 tablespoon fresh lemon juice
1 teaspoon vanilla extract
2 cups water

1 **For Crust:** Grease a 7" springform pan and set aside.

2 Add vanilla wafers and almonds to a food processor. Pulse to combine. Add in melted butter and pulse to blend. Transfer crumb mixture to springform pan and press down along the bottom and about ⅓ of the way up the sides of the pan. Place a square of aluminum foil along the outside of the bottom of the pan and crimp up around the edges.

3 **For Cheesecake Filling:** With a hand blender or food processor, cream together cream cheese, sour cream, and sugar. Pulse until smooth. Slowly add eggs, lemon zest, lemon juice, and vanilla extract. Pulse for another 10 seconds. Scrape the bowl and pulse until batter is smooth.

4 Transfer the batter into springform pan.

5 Pour the water into the Instant Pot®. Insert the trivet. Set the springform pan on the trivet. Lock lid.

6 Press the Manual button and adjust time to 30 minutes. When the timer beeps, quick-release pressure until float valve drops and then unlock lid. Lift pan out of Instant Pot®. Let cool at room temperature for 10 minutes.

7 The cheesecake will be a little jiggly in the center. Refrigerate for a minimum of 2 hours to allow it to set. Release side pan and serve.

Spiced Red Wine-Poached Pears

Impress your guests with this elegant, beautiful, and tasty dessert. And feel free to mix things up—use Bartlett, Anjou, or Bosc pears. Just find the best one that is ripe but still firm. Then elevate this dish before serving with a scoop of vanilla or cinnamon ice cream.

- **Hands-On Time: 15 minutes**
- **Cook Time: 13 minutes**

Serves 4

4 ripe but still firm pears

2 tablespoons fresh lemon juice

4 cups dry red wine

½ cup freshly squeezed orange juice

2 teaspoons grated orange zest

¼ cup sugar

1 cinnamon stick

½ teaspoon ground cloves

½ teaspoon ground ginger

1 sprig fresh mint

1 Rinse and peel the pears leaving the stem. Using a corer or melon baller, remove the cores from underneath without going through the top so you can maintain the stem. Brush the pears inside and out with the lemon juice.

2 Combine the wine, orange juice, orange zest, sugar, cinnamon stick, cloves, and ginger in Instant Pot®. Press the Sauté button and then hit the Adjust button to change the temperature to More. Bring to a slow boil in about 3–5 minutes; stir to blend and dissolve the sugar. Carefully place the pears in liquid. Press Adjust button to change temperature to Less and simmer unlidded for 5 additional minutes. Lock lid.

3 Press Manual button and adjust time to 3 minutes. Use the Pressure button to set the pressure to Low. When the timer beeps, quick-release pressure until float valve drops and then unlock lid.

4 Use a slotted spoon to transfer the pears to a serving platter. Garnish with mint sprig.

Peanut Butter Chocolate Cheesecake

Save the decadence of this rich dessert for special occasions. Creamy peanut butter cheesecake topped with chocolate chips and nuts is a winning combination. Finishing it off with a chocolate drizzle and fresh whipped cream only increases the wow factor.

- **Hands-On Time: 10 minutes**
- **Cook Time: 30 minutes**

Serves 6

Crust

20 vanilla wafers
2 tablespoons creamy peanut butter
3 tablespoons melted butter

Cheesecake Filling

12 ounces cream cheese, cubed and room temperature
2 tablespoons sour cream, room temperature
½ cup sugar
¼ cup unsweetened cocoa
2 large eggs, room temperature
1 teaspoon vanilla extract
2 cups water
¼ cup mini semisweet chocolate chips
¼ cup chopped peanuts
2 tablespoons chocolate syrup
1 cup whipped cream

1 **For Crust:** Grease a 7" springform pan and set aside.

2 Add vanilla wafers to a food processor and pulse to combine. Add in peanut butter and melted butter. Pulse to blend. Transfer crumb mixture to springform pan and press down along the bottom and about ⅓ of the way up the sides of the pan. Place a square of aluminum foil along the outside bottom of the pan and crimp up around the edges.

3 **For Cheesecake Filling:** With a hand blender or food processor, cream together cream cheese, sour cream, sugar, and cocoa. Pulse until smooth. Slowly add eggs and vanilla extract. Pulse for another 10 seconds. Scrape the bowl and pulse until batter is smooth. Transfer the batter into springform pan.

4 Pour water into the Instant Pot®. Insert the trivet. Set the springform pan on the trivet. Lock lid.

5 Press the Manual button and adjust time to 30 minutes. When timer beeps, quick-release pressure until float valve drops and then unlock lid. Lift pan out of Instant Pot®. Garnish immediately with chocolate chips and chopped peanuts. Let cool at room temperature for 10 minutes.

6 The cheesecake will be a little jiggly in the center. Refrigerate for a minimum of 2 hours to allow it to set. Release side pan and serve with drizzled chocolate syrup and whipped cream.

Pumpkin Cheesecake

Every October, no matter which way you turn, pumpkin takes over the food world. Unfortunately, most pumpkin products are full of processed ingredients and flavorings. This cheesecake uses real pumpkin purée and is the perfect-sized bite of cheesecake without overindulging in such a decadent dessert.

- **Hands-On Time: 10 minutes**
- **Cook Time: 30 minutes**

Serves 6

Crust
20 gingersnaps
3 tablespoons melted butter

Cheesecake Filling
1 cup pumpkin purée
8 ounces cream cheese, cubed and room temperature
2 tablespoons sour cream, room temperature
½ cup sugar
Pinch of salt
2 large eggs, room temperature
¼ teaspoon ground cinnamon
⅛ teaspoon ground nutmeg
½ teaspoon vanilla extract
2 cups water

1. Grease a 7" springform pan and set aside.

2. **For Crust:** Add gingersnaps to a food processor and pulse to combine. Add in melted butter and pulse to blend. Transfer crumb mixture to springform pan and press down along the bottom and about ⅓ of the way up the sides of the pan. Place a square of aluminum foil along the outside bottom of the pan and crimp up around the edges.

3. **For Cheesecake Filling:** With a hand blender or food processor, cream together pumpkin, cream cheese, sour cream, sugar, and salt. Pulse until smooth. Slowly add eggs, cinnamon, nutmeg, and vanilla. Pulse for another 10 seconds. Scrape the bowl and pulse until batter is smooth.

4. Transfer the batter into springform pan.

5. Pour water into the Instant Pot®. Insert the trivet. Set the springform pan on the trivet. Lock lid.

6. Press the Manual button and adjust time to 30 minutes. When timer beeps, quick-release pressure until float valve drops and then unlock lid. Lift pan out of Instant Pot®. Let cool at room temperature for 10 minutes.

7. The cheesecake will be a little jiggly in the center. Refrigerate for a minimum of 2 hours to allow it to set. Release side pan and serve.

White Chocolate Pots de Crème

It is so amazing how simple ingredients like eggs, sugar, and milk can create such pure delight. It's even more amazing that the Instant Pot® is a cooking vessel that is able to steam this custard to perfection.

- **Hands-On Time: 15 minutes**
- **Cook Time: 20 minutes**

Serves 4

4 large egg yolks
2 tablespoons sugar
Pinch of salt
¼ teaspoon vanilla extract
1½ cups half-and-half
¾ cup white chocolate chips
2 cups water

1 In a small bowl, whisk together egg yolks, sugar, salt, and vanilla. Set aside.

2 In saucepan over medium-low heat, heat half-and-half to a low simmer. Whisk a spoonful into the egg mixture to temper the eggs, and then slowly whisk that egg mixture into the saucepan with remaining half-and-half. Add white chocolate chips and continually stir on simmer until chocolate is melted, about 10 minutes. Remove from heat and evenly distribute white chocolate mixture among four custard ramekins.

3 Pour water into Instant Pot®. Insert trivet. Place silicone steamer basket onto trivet. Place ramekins onto steamer basket. Lock lid.

4 Press the Manual button and adjust time to 6 minutes. When timer beeps, let pressure release naturally for 10 minutes. Quick-release any additional pressure until float valve drops and then unlock lid.

5 Transfer custards to a plate and refrigerate covered for 2 hours. Serve.

Chocolate Custard

Baked in individual ramekins, this super silky dessert will hit the spot. Chocolatey goodness is always popular, and with the Instant Pot®, it's also easy to make. The egg yolks used in this recipe give it a creaminess and custard-like texture that you're sure to love. Serve chilled with a dollop of fresh whipped cream.

- **Hands-On Time: 15 minutes**
- **Cook Time: 20 minutes**

Serves 4

4 large egg yolks
2 tablespoons sugar
Pinch of salt
¼ teaspoon vanilla extract
1½ cups half-and-half
¾ cup semisweet chocolate chips
2 cups water

1 In a small bowl, whisk together egg yolks, sugar, salt, and vanilla. Set aside.

2 In saucepan over medium-low heat, heat half-and-half to a low simmer. Whisk a spoonful into the egg mixture to temper the eggs, then slowly add the egg mixture back into the saucepan with remaining half-and-half. Add chocolate chips and continually stir on simmer until chocolate is melted, about 10 minutes. Remove from heat and evenly distribute chocolate mixture among four custard ramekins.

3 Pour water into Instant Pot®. Insert trivet. Place silicone steamer basket onto trivet. Place ramekins onto steamer basket. Lock lid.

4 Press the Manual button and adjust time to 6 minutes. When timer beeps, let pressure release naturally for 10 minutes. Quick-release any additional pressure until float valve drops and then unlock lid.

5 Transfer custards to a plate and refrigerate covered for 2 hours. Serve.

Butterscotch Crème Brûlée

Not that you need an excuse to break out the blowtorch, but if one were ever needed, it is with this decadent dessert. The Instant Pot® removes any intimidation you may feel about this French classic, and the taste is well worth it as well. So put on your beret and get to torching!

- **Hands-On Time: 15 minutes**
- **Cook Time: 20 minutes**

Serves 4

4 large egg yolks
2 tablespoons sugar
Pinch of salt
¼ teaspoon vanilla extract
1½ cups half-and-half
¾ cup butterscotch chips
2 cups water
½ cup superfine sugar

1 In a small bowl, whisk together egg yolks, sugar, salt, and vanilla. Set aside.

2 In saucepan over medium-low heat, heat half-and-half until you reach a low simmer. Whisk a spoonful into the egg mixture to temper the eggs, then slowly add the egg mixture back into the saucepan with remaining half-and-half. Add butterscotch chips and continually stir on simmer until butterscotch is melted, about 10 minutes. Remove from heat and evenly distribute butterscotch mixture among four custard ramekins.

3 Pour water into Instant Pot®. Insert trivet. Place silicone steamer basket onto trivet. Place ramekins onto steamer basket. Lock lid.

4 Press the Manual button and adjust time to 6 minutes. When the timer beeps, let pressure release naturally for 10 minutes. Quick-release any additional pressure until float valve drops and then unlock lid.

5 Transfer custards to a plate and refrigerate covered for 2 hours.

6 Right before serving, top custards with equal amounts superfine sugar. Blow-torch the tops to create a caramelized shell. Serve.

Superfine Sugar

Superfine sugar is smaller than granulated sugar and is sold in most specialty stores. You can also just pulse regular sugar in a food processor to achieve the same results.

Cornmeal Cake

Cornmeal in cake? It sounds odd, but actually the sweetness from the cornmeal makes this the perfect decision. Enjoy for dessert or even as a little sweet bite with your cup of tea or coffee in the morning.

- **Hands-On Time: 5 minutes**
- **Cook Time: 20 minutes**

Serves 6

2 cups milk
¼ cup packed light brown sugar
1 teaspoon orange zest
½ cup self-rising cornmeal
1 large egg
2 egg yolks
2 tablespoons melted butter
2 tablespoons orange marmalade
1 cup water

1 Heat the milk in a saucepan over medium heat until it reaches a simmer. Stir in the brown sugar; simmer and stir until the milk is at a low boil, about 2–3 minutes. Whisk in the orange zest and cornmeal. Simmer and stir for 2 minutes or until thickened. Remove from heat.

2 In a small bowl, whisk together egg, egg yolks, butter, and orange marmalade. Add a spoonful of the cornmeal mixture into the egg mixture and quickly stir to temper the eggs. Slowly add the egg mixture into the cornmeal mixture.

3 Grease a 6" baking pan. Transfer the cornmeal batter to the prepared pan.

4 Pour water into Instant Pot® and insert trivet. Place the cake pan on trivet. Lock lid.

5 Press the Manual button and adjust time to 15 minutes. When timer beeps, quick-release pressure until float valve drops and then unlock lid. Transfer cake pan to a cooling rack. Serve when cooled.

Creamy Key Lime Pie

Although a "regular" or Persian lime can be used in this dish, key limes are known for their distinct flavor, stronger aroma, and tartness. The juxtaposition of the creamy and tart in this pie will have you going back for a second and third piece. Luckily, the practical size of this dessert doesn't allow you to get you too far off track while satisfying that sweet tooth.

- **Hands-On Time: 10 minutes**
- **Cook Time: 30 minutes**

Serves 6

Crust
6 crushed graham crackers (about 1 cup)
3 tablespoons melted butter

Key Lime Filling
12 ounces cream cheese, cubed and room temperature
2 tablespoons sour cream, room temperature
½ cup sugar
2 large eggs, room temperature
Zest of 4 key limes, grated
1 tablespoon fresh key lime juice
1 teaspoon vanilla extract
2 cups water

1 **For Crust:** Grease a 7" springform pan and set aside.

2 Pulse graham crackers in a food processor. Add in melted butter and pulse to blend. Transfer crumb mixture to springform pan and press down along the bottom and about ⅓ of the way up the sides of the pan. Place a square of aluminum foil along the outside bottom of the pan and crimp up around the edges.

3 **For Key Lime Filling:** With food processor, pulse together cream cheese, sour cream, and sugar until smooth. Slowly add eggs, key lime zest, key lime juice, and vanilla. Pulse for another 10 seconds. Scrape the edges of the bowl and pulse until batter is smooth.

4 Transfer the batter into springform pan.

5 **To Finish:** Pour the water into the Instant Pot®. Insert the trivet. Set the springform pan on the trivet. Lock lid.

6 Press the Manual button and adjust time to 30 minutes. When timer beeps, quick-release pressure until float valve drops and then unlock lid. Lift pan out of Instant Pot®. Let cool at room temperature for 10 minutes.

7 The cheesecake will be a little jiggly in the center. Refrigerate for a minimum of 2 hours to continue to allow it to set. Release side pan and serve.

Pearberry Crisp

This delicious Pearberry Crisp is the perfect pick-me-up for those down days when you just need something sweet. Scoop this right out of the Instant Pot® and into your bowl. Top with vanilla or cinnamon ice cream, or even some fresh whipped cream. This is sure to cure any blues that may be ailing you.

- **Hands-On Time: 15 minutes**
- **Cook Time: 8 minutes**

Serves 4

Pearberry Filling

6 medium pears, peeled, cored, and diced
1 cup thawed frozen mixed berries
¼ cup water
1 tablespoon fresh lemon juice
2 tablespoons pure maple syrup
1 teaspoon ground cinnamon
¼ teaspoon ground nutmeg
Pinch of salt

Topping

4 tablespoons melted butter
1 cup old-fashioned oats
⅛ cup all-purpose flour
¼ cup chopped almonds
¼ cup packed light brown sugar
¼ teaspoon sea salt

1 **For Pearberry Filling:** Place Pearberry Filling ingredients in Instant Pot®. Stir to distribute ingredients.

2 **For Topping:** Mix Topping ingredients together in a small bowl. Spoon drops of topping over the filling. Lock lid.

3 Press the Manual button and adjust time to 8 minutes. When the timer beeps, let pressure release naturally until float valve drops and then unlock lid. Spoon into bowls and enjoy.

Carrot Coconut Cake

The coconut flavor in this cake lends a little extra to the traditional carrot cake. This is the perfect-sized cake for a romantic dinner or even when you have a stop-by guest wanting a little tea and gossip. For some extra zip, toast some coconut flakes and use them to garnish the top of the cake after frosting.

- **Hands-On Time: 10 minutes**
- **Cook Time: 20 minutes**

Serves 4

¼ cup coconut oil, melted
½ cup sugar
1 large egg
½ teaspoon ground cinnamon
Pinch of ground nutmeg
½ teaspoon vanilla extract
¼ cup peeled, grated carrot
¼ cup unsweetened coconut flakes
½ cup all-purpose flour
½ teaspoon baking powder
¼ cup chopped pecans
1 cup water

1 In a medium bowl, whisk together oil, sugar, egg, cinnamon, nutmeg, vanilla, carrot, coconut flakes, flour, and baking powder. Do not overmix. Fold in pecans. Pour batter into a greased 6" cake pan.

2 Pour water into the Instant Pot®. Set trivet in pot. Place cake pan on top of the trivet. Lock lid.

3 Press the Manual button and adjust time to 20 minutes. When timer beeps, let pressure release naturally for 5 minutes. Quick-release any additional pressure until float valve drops and then unlock lid.

4 Remove cake pan from the pot and transfer to a rack until cool. Flip cake onto a serving platter.

INSTANT POT® OPTIONS
Blend the following ingredients together to create a homemade Cream Cheese Frosting for this adorable cake: 4 ounces (½ block) of cream cheese at room temperature, ½ cup softened butter, ½ teaspoon vanilla extract, 8 tablespoons powdered sugar, and just a pinch of salt.

Festive Fruitcake

There's no need to regift this dish as your guests will be astonished that they actually like fruitcake. You may even want to try using some mini loaf pans in the Instant Pot® to create some small red-ribbon gifts that are perfect for coworkers, teachers, or anyone else you want to appreciate. There are 5.75" loaf pans available, so you would have to make these one at a time, but they would fit!

- **Hands-On Time: 15 minutes**
- **Cook Time: 20 minutes**

Serves 8

1 (8-ounce) can crushed
   pineapple, including juice
½ cup raisins
½ cup dried unsweetened
   cherries
½ cup pitted and diced dates
1 cup pecan halves
½ cup chopped walnuts
½ cup unsweetened coconut
   flakes
½ cup sugar
¼ cup melted butter, cooled
2 teaspoons vanilla extract
2 tablespoons fresh orange
   juice
4 large eggs
1 cup all-purpose flour
2 teaspoons baking powder
¼ teaspoon salt
¼ teaspoon ground nutmeg
1 cup water

1 In a medium bowl, combine all ingredients except water until well mixed. Grease a 6" cake pan. Press mixture into the pan.

2 Pour 1 cup water into the Instant Pot®. Insert trivet. Lower 6" pan onto trivet. Lock lid.

3 Press the Manual button and adjust time to 20 minutes. When timer beeps, let pressure release naturally for 10 minutes. Quick-release any additional pressure until float valve drops and then unlock lid.

4 Remove fruitcake from Instant Pot® and transfer to a cooling rack. Refrigerate covered overnight. Flip onto a cutting board, slice, and serve.

Why Fruitcake?

The poor fruitcake. It has been regifted and snubbed for years. So why do we keep making it and passing it along to our loved ones? For the haters, this question is asked each year on cue. But, for the lovers of this confection, the joy of this dish dates back to the Romans. Filled with nuts, fruit, sugar, and, most importantly, tradition, the fruitcake is around to stay!

Steamed Bread Pudding

This recipe can be changed up so many ways, so once you get the hang of the dish, feel free to make it your own. Use whatever bread you have on hand. Add some chopped nuts. In Puerto Rico, the bread is soaked in coconut milk. Substitute dried pineapple for the raisins (or just add them in!), and you'll have a completely different recipe on your hands each time.

- **Hands-On Time: 10 minutes**
- **Cook Time: 20 minutes**

Serves 6

4 cups cubed cinnamon-raisin bread, dried out overnight

1 apple, peeled, cored, and diced small

¼ cup raisins

2 cups whole milk

3 large eggs

½ teaspoon vanilla extract

2 tablespoons pure maple syrup

¼ teaspoon ground cinnamon

Pinch of ground nutmeg

Pinch of sea salt

3 tablespoons butter, cut into 3 pats

1½ cups water

1 Grease a 7-cup glass dish. Add bread, apple, and raisins. Set aside.

2 In a small bowl, whisk together milk, eggs, vanilla, maple syrup, cinnamon, nutmeg, and salt. Pour over bread in glass dish and place pats of butter on top.

3 Pour water into Instant Pot®. Set trivet in pot. Place glass dish on top of trivet. Lock lid.

4 Press the Manual button and adjust time to 20 minutes. When timer beeps, quick-release pressure until float valve drops and then unlock lid.

5 Remove glass bowl from the Instant Pot®. Transfer to a rack until cooled. Serve.

Cinnamon Brown Rice Pudding

Classic, creamy, and bursting with soothing flavors, this spiced rice pudding can be prepared quickly—and eaten slowly. Enjoy this comforting dessert at the end of a hard day or even as a warming breakfast on those cold mornings when something boring just won't do.

- **Hands-On Time: 5 minutes**
- **Cook Time: 25 minutes**

Serves 4

1 cup short-grain brown rice
1⅓ cups water
1 tablespoon vanilla extract
1 cinnamon stick
1 tablespoon butter
1 cup raisins
3 tablespoons honey
½ cup heavy cream

1 Add rice, water, vanilla, cinnamon stick, and butter to Instant Pot®. Lock lid.

2 Press the Manual button and adjust time to 20 minutes. When timer beeps, let pressure release naturally for 10 minutes. Quick-release any additional pressure until float valve drops and then unlock lid.

3 Remove the cinnamon stick and discard. Stir in the raisins, honey, and cream.

4 Press Sauté button on Instant Pot®, press Adjust button to change the temperature to Less, and simmer unlidded for 5 minutes. Serve warm.

Nutty Brownie Cake

This Nutty Brownie Cake is a perfect slice of perfection when you are craving something chocolate. With its small stature, this recipe will fulfill that sweet tooth without leaving evidence in the morning. Cook it and you're done. Tomorrow is a new day.

- **Hands-On Time: 10 minutes**
- **Cook Time: 20 minutes**

Serves 6

4 tablespoons butter, room temperature

2 large eggs

⅓ cup all-purpose flour

½ teaspoon baking powder

⅓ cup unsweetened cocoa powder

Pinch of sea salt

⅓ cup sugar

⅓ cup semisweet chocolate chips

⅓ cup chopped pecans

1 cup water

2 tablespoons powdered sugar

1 In a large bowl, whisk together butter, eggs, flour, baking powder, cocoa powder, salt, and sugar. Do not overmix. Fold in chocolate chips and pecans. Pour batter into a greased 6" cake pan. Cover pan with a piece of aluminum foil.

2 Pour water into the Instant Pot®. Set trivet in pot. Place cake pan on top of the trivet. Lock lid.

3 Press the Manual button and adjust time to 20 minutes. When timer beeps, let pressure release naturally for 5 minutes. Quick-release any additional pressure until float valve drops and then unlock lid.

4 Remove cake pan from the Instant Pot® and transfer to a rack to cool. Sprinkle with powdered sugar and serve.

Smash Cake Pan

Traditionally, a 6" smash cake pan is what is used to cook the cake for the first birthday of a child with the perceived result that the child will smash the cake in his/her face for an excellent photo opportunity. It is also the perfect-sized pan to fit into an Instant Pot®. You can find this size of cake pan in some specialty stores and also online. If you are addicted to your Instant Pot® and want a small cake from time to time, get this pan.

Pineapple Upside-Down Cake

Traditional pineapple upside-down cakes use sliced pineapples, but because this is a 6"
pan, crushed pineapple is a perfect substitute. You can also have fun and get creative with
the cherries used in this dish. Make a heart for Valentine's Day or create whatever pattern
your imagination can conceive.

- **Hands-On Time: 5 minutes**
- **Cook Time: 35 minutes**

Serves 4

½ cup drained crushed
    pineapple
12 maraschino cherries
1 large egg
2 tablespoons melted butter
⅓ cup sugar
1 teaspoon vanilla extract
1 cup ricotta cheese
1 cup flour
2 teaspoons baking powder
1 teaspoon baking soda
Pinch of salt
1½ cups water

1   Grease a 6" cake pan. Place a circle of parchment paper in the bottom. Add a layer of pineapple and distribute cherries evenly among the pineapple.

2   In a medium bowl, beat egg. Whisk in butter, sugar, and vanilla until smooth. Add remaining ingredients except water. Pour into pan over pineapple and cherries.

3   Pour water into Instant Pot®. Add trivet. Lower cake pan onto trivet. Lock lid.

4   Press the Manual button and adjust time to 35 minutes. When the timer beeps, quick-release pressure until float valve drops and then unlock lid.

5   Remove cake pan from the pot and transfer to a rack to cool. Flip cake onto a serving platter. Remove parchment paper. Slice and serve.

Spiced Peaches with Cinnamon Whipped Cream

When you need a quick dessert and you have to shop in your pantry for ingredients, this dessert is for you. Keep a couple of cans of peaches ready for when your sweet tooth strikes. Most of the other ingredients are typical in households. The whipped cream is optional but is the proverbial cherry on top!

- **Hands-On Time: 15 minutes**
- **Cook Time: 8 minutes**

Serves 6

1½ cups heavy whipping cream

2 tablespoons powdered sugar

1 teaspoon ground cinnamon

½ teaspoon vanilla extract

2 (15-ounce) cans sliced peaches in syrup

¼ cup water

2 tablespoons packed light brown sugar

1 tablespoon white wine vinegar

⅛ teaspoon ground allspice

1 teaspoon ground ginger

1 cinnamon stick

4 whole cloves

Pinch of cayenne pepper

3 whole black peppercorns

1. Pour whipping cream into a metal bowl. Whisk until soft peaks form. Slowly add powdered sugar, cinnamon, and vanilla and continue whipping until firm. Set aside and refrigerate.

2. Add remaining ingredients to Instant Pot®. Stir to mix. Lock lid.

3. Press the Manual button and adjust time to 3 minutes. When timer beeps, quick-release pressure until float valve drops and then unlock lid. Remove and discard the cinnamon stick, cloves, and peppercorns. Press Sauté button on Instant Pot®, press Adjust button to change the temperature to Less, and simmer for 5 minutes to thicken the syrup. Serve warm or chilled, topped with cinnamon whipped cream.

U.S./Metric Conversion Chart

VOLUME CONVERSIONS

U.S. Volume Measure	Metric Equivalent
⅛ teaspoon	0.5 milliliter
¼ teaspoon	1 milliliter
½ teaspoon	2 milliliters
1 teaspoon	5 milliliters
½ tablespoon	7 milliliters
1 tablespoon (3 teaspoons)	15 milliliters
2 tablespoons (1 fluid ounce)	30 milliliters
¼ cup (4 tablespoons)	60 milliliters
⅓ cup	90 milliliters
½ cup (4 fluid ounces)	125 milliliters
⅔ cup	160 milliliters
¾ cup (6 fluid ounces)	180 milliliters
1 cup (16 tablespoons)	250 milliliters
1 pint (2 cups)	500 milliliters
1 quart (4 cups)	1 liter (about)

WEIGHT CONVERSIONS

U.S. Weight Measure	Metric Equivalent
½ ounce	15 grams
1 ounce	30 grams
2 ounces	60 grams
3 ounces	85 grams
¼ pound (4 ounces)	115 grams
½ pound (8 ounces)	225 grams
¾ pound (12 ounces)	340 grams
1 pound (16 ounces)	454 grams

OVEN TEMPERATURE CONVERSIONS

Degrees Fahrenheit	Degrees Celsius
200 degrees F	95 degrees C
250 degrees F	120 degrees C
275 degrees F	135 degrees C
300 degrees F	150 degrees C
325 degrees F	160 degrees C
350 degrees F	180 degrees C
375 degrees F	190 degrees C
400 degrees F	205 degrees C
425 degrees F	220 degrees C
450 degrees F	230 degrees C

BAKING PAN SIZES

American	Metric
8 x 1½ inch round baking pan	20 x 4 cm cake tin
9 x 1½ inch round baking pan	23 x 3.5 cm cake tin
11 x 7 x 1½ inch baking pan	28 x 18 x 4 cm baking tin
13 x 9 x 2 inch baking pan	30 x 20 x 5 cm baking tin
2 quart rectangular baking dish	30 x 20 x 3 cm baking tin
15 x 10 x 2 inch baking pan	30 x 25 x 2 cm baking tin (Swiss roll tin)
9 inch pie plate	22 x 4 or 23 x 4 cm pie plate
7 or 8 inch springform pan	18 or 20 cm springform or loose bottom cake tin
9 x 5 x 3 inch loaf pan	23 x 13 x 7 cm or 2 lb narrow loaf or pate tin
1½ quart casserole	1.5 liter casserole
2 quart casserole	2 liter casserole

Paleo and Gluten-Free Recipes

Index

Note: Page numbers in *italics* indicate recipe photos.

About the Author

Michelle Fagone is a recipe developer, mother of two, and food blogger. On her site, CavegirlCuisine.com, Michelle shares recipes and knowledge about the health benefits of cooking with local, fresh, and unprocessed foods. Despite being a southern gal at heart, her travel and food experiences as a Navy brat and current Army spouse have given her a unique appreciation for worldly flavors. While comfort is the basis for most of her recipes, you will often find a twist of exciting flavors and combinations that make her recipes not only appealing to a broad audience, but uniquely delicious! *Cavegirl Cuisine* was named one of the Top 50 Paleo Blogs of 2012 by the Institute for the Psychology of Eating. She lives in Louisville, Kentucky.